The
Mini-Atlas of
CATS

Andrew De Prisco
and
James B. Johnson

TS-152

Featured Photographer:
Isabelle Français

Additional Photography: Dr. Herbert R. Axelrod, Victor Baldwin, Paul Casey, Cora Cobb, Donna J. Coss, Barry B. Dowe, Jal Duncan, Jack B. Fischer, Dorothy Holby, Brian Kahof, Gillian Lisle, Roger Michael, Pete Miller, Ray Paulsen, Robert Pearcy, Ron Reagan, D.H. Shagam, Vince Serbin, Skotzke and Lucas Photography, Sally Anne Thompson.

Title page: Black Devon Rex, owned by Mary Theresa and Joel Singer.

Distributed in the UNITED STATES by T.F.H. Publications, Inc., One T.F.H. Plaza, Neptune City, NJ 07753; in CANADA to the Pet Trade by H & L Pet Supplies Inc., 27 Kingston Crescent, Kitchener, Ontario N2B 2T6; Rolf C. Hagen Ltd., 3225 Sartelon Street, Montreal 382 Quebec; in CANADA to the Book Trade by Macmillan of Canada (A Division of Canada Publishing Corporation), 164 Commander Boulevard, Agincourt, Ontario M1S 3C7; in ENGLAND by T.F.H. Publications, PO Box 15, Waterlooville PO7 6BQ; in AUSTRALIA AND THE SOUTH PACIFIC by T.F.H. (Australia) Pty. Ltd., Box 149, Brookvale 2100 N.S.W., Australia; in NEW ZEALAND by Ross Haines & Son, Ltd., 82 D Elizabeth Knox Place, Panmure, Auckland, New Zealand; in the PHILIPPINES by Bio-Research, 5 Lippay Street, San Lorenzo Village, Makati, Rizal; in SOUTH AFRICA by Multipet Pty. Ltd., P.O. Box 35347, Northway, 4065, South Africa. Published by T.F.H. Publications, Inc. Manufactured in the United States of America by T.F.H. Publications, Inc.

The
Mini-Atlas of
CATS

Andrew De Prisco
and
James B. Johnson

Contents

Foreword

Cat haters can't be converted: so many good reasons to hate a cat. Admitted hateful *Homo sapiens*, ablurred in the glassy black-hearted eyes of the cat, are taken aback by the mutual abhorrence sketched by the feline's well-honed claws—its swords of uncivil disobedience unfurled in its woods of peed-on petunias.

Petunia-keeping cat haters trowel the plots of these leisure-seeking freedom abusers who define themselves by perpetual unemployment, dumb whims and nasty moods. Dog-keeping cat haters hose these arched-backed archenemies of their well-domesticated canine.

Touched and untouchable, smugly condescending, feline houseguests courteously exhibit a lack of gratitude, and a smidgeon of spite.

With spit and with spite—scornful, willful—flea-ridden fat cats devour helpless prey, baby prey, canaries and gerbils, innocents that have conceded (without spite) to domestication.

Why do people hate cats?? What attributes of the cat do people recognize as their own?: The tactless tactics of taxing sex? Unreserved, untacit, untiring . . . emoting, emitting . . . agape-mouthed, eros-consumed sensualists. Lazy, standoffish loiterers/litterers, in plush retirement. Voracious, insistent, snobbish, independent: How enviable to be a cat! Shameless Cat, sinful Man (?).

Kaleidoscopes of cats to be burned, drowned, abandoned, poached, and impounded: spellbound blacks that mar man's good paths; unsound whites that shatter well-drummed breeding plans; vicious AOCs that reopen childhood scars; plucky marbled and striped thousand-pounders that pillage hens and men; motley mottled moggies that litter the tidy lane.

Historically humans have exercised great inconsistency in their treatment of the cat—the holy lion to the hunted cougar. Are we to muse over the feline's distrust and distaste for the human race?

Musing colorblind unseeing humans render the unfeeling feline in their own gray terms so that they can despise it with proper justification. Collaring the cat into submission, we nurture its dependence and childlike behavior, re-thinking its motives and actions. With psychoanalytical desperation, we attempt to understand the feline id, decode and recode, label, classify—then tame, train, groom and bridle.

Humans clash with cats because both species are curious and persistent.

Cats, however, exert minimal energy toward understanding humans, content to be different, nonspecific, indifferent . . . Hate requires much too much energy for a cat—indifference is energy-smart.

Energetic cat haters and lovers insist on undermining or understanding the cat. The authors, despite the cat's indifference and lack of enthusiasm, enjoy thinking and writing about the cat, our most comical, easy-to-hate, easy-to-love fellow creature. This hate–love relationship fascinates humans and provokes the authorship and purchase of books. Whether you pitch your pup-tent in the camp of the ailurophobes or -philes, we, the impulsive, feline-adoring authors, hope that you find this *Mini-Atlas* both worthwhile and enjoyable, and beg the mauled reader's patience in this torturously tortuous literary cat and mouse game.

Source materials and field work for this little book are indebted to the cats we have known, the cat lovers we have pestered, the cat haters we have lynched, and the fellow authors we have pinched.

A.D./J.J.

Dedication

To our parents,
Louie and Doris
Jim and Barbara.
Special cats in our lives,
Puffy, Tiffany, Pumpkin (Red)
and Kitty.

Andrew and Jim

The authors wish to acknowledge in particular the photographer Isabelle Français, for her outstanding talent and continued dedication to her work. Special thanks to Deirdre Connelly for much-needed guidance.

We are also proud to feature exclusively the wild cat paintings of John R. Quinn, a fine artist and human being.

'D<small>ID</small> <small>YOU</small> <small>SAY</small> <small>PIG,</small> <small>OR</small> <small>FIG?</small>' <small>SAID</small> <small>THE</small> C<small>AT.</small>

L<small>EWIS</small> C<small>ARROLL</small>

Why a Cat?

Idiosyncrasies, out of sync with the household over which they exceptionlessly rule, are more the rule and less the exception. Cats remain unpredictable yet very routine, abundantly affectionate yet mostly independent and self-reliant; balancing the

Bringing to light all of the nuances of its feline personality, this phosphorescent adolescent assumes a shady post. Bombay owned by Janet Becker.

innocence of a newborn, the curiosity of an adolescent and the indifference and jadedness of a tribe's elder, cats have monopolized and molded man's fascination.

Observing the cat piques man's interest on many different levels: the physical, psychological, and instinctual. The feline physique, in both domestic and wild cats, is singular in its efficiency, grace and perfection. The cat's ability to communicate with others of its species and with man is reliant on its senses and instincts.

The uniqueness of felines is not reserved to the great ones: the lion, tiger and puma. Instead, we will see how all cats, whether 500 pounds or five pounds, essentially behave the same. It is the awesome instincts and behavioral patterns of wild felines that attract many people to owning a domestic cat. The majority of the human population cannot resist the majesty or charm of the big cats, as any zookeeper will graciously concede. So much of feline behavior is universal to all cats, as we will see.

Not amused or impressed by the ethological assumptions and verbal antics of men, the jaguar remains aloof.

LINKS TO THE LION AND THE LYNX

The cat's territory, without need of lease or deed, is transient and inviolable; the sacred possession is defined by the cat because it happens to stand where it stands—not necessarily the domestic

Blue-eyed Longhairs have a long history of assailing ceramic wilds, with little regard for their own safety.

cat's real estate or the wild cat's "neck of the woods." Time of day or night, the need for space, this moment's whim all fix loosely a cat's territory. The purpose of survival, personal and species, is connected to this inherent struggle.

While domestic cats do not face the same ecological needs that wild cats do, they still have strong territorial instincts. In the wild, the male cat must define its territory for its survival, the sustaining of its source of food and shelter. The lion uniquely defends its territory as the sanctuary of its pride, its mates and young. Wandering neighborhood toms are more or less aggressive depending on how close they are to home. House cats defend two areas as their turf. Area number one, the home itself, is the cat's castle; when it is close to it, its aggressiveness towers. The second area is loosely sketched by the cat itself to include any place it frequents on its way to and from area number one. It is these places that the cat may or may not defend, depending on its mood on the given day and the size of the particular intruder.

The angry roar and snarl of a defending lion or jaguar make quiver the surrounding mountains; so too do the amplified growls and hisses of two domestic toms rolling on a neighbor's stoop make rattle the surrounding mailboxes. Such hair-raising outbursts—cats are horribly fond of drama—are as ritualized as any ancient Greek cere-

Vocalizing the ground rules, a pride of female lions assures maned passers-by of prenuptial expectations.

How apt your domestic will be to voice its opinions and expectations varies from breed to breed. The Somali, the longhaired cousin to the Abyssinian, is often "ruddy" to speak up. Owner, Gale Taylor.

mony or professional wrestling match. The aggressor cat will erect his back fur and bush out his tail, stretch his head forward, spreading his ears outward, growl, yowl, slobber, spit and hiss. His opponent, in good course, will do a close impersonation of his now contorted and ugly feline aggressor. Direct eye contact, usually avoided in the cat community, intensifies and communicates the tom's outrage. The tumble ceremony is initiated by the cats' ambling pad by pad towards each other, head to head, until they are abreast; they then prepare to spring, and freeze. (The freeze is undoubtedly for dramatic effect, as each cat beholds the full realm of its opponent's spit and groaning resonance.) Dripping mouths, whipping tails, and unwavering stares, the cats then spring, claw, bite, grope, hit, grab (a dastardly sight assuredly). This tumble is repeated until one (smart, though defeated) cat decides not to re-enter the "ring."

Typically having less-expansive territories than the broad-ranging males, female cats are also known to protect their territory but they are more judicious and compromising than the narrow-minded neighborhood toms. Females will adhere to a semi-agreed-upon schedule of the same territory with other cats so as to evade possible altercations.

Like the great cats, neighborhood cats do not prefer to fight, even though they are well equipped to do so. The cat surely prefers

A dozing tabby embarking on an afternoon nap.

The European wild cat, also called the forest wild cat, secludes itself in the tree of its choice. Despite the close family resemblance to the domestic cat and its sleepy docility, this tot of a wild is extremely vicious.

peace and serenity to commotion and a scratched nose. Cat owners take into consideration the feline's strong territorial instincts when introducing a new cat (or dog, bite your tongue) to the household. The home, as the cat's principal territory, is unlikely to be shared willingly by your cat. Eventually, the older cat will compromise and delineate a few centimeters to the new family pet. In many instances, the older cat harbors resentment for the new animal and will never become completely accepting. Often the cats will show dominance or subordination in ways too subtle for an unknowing human to perceive. (Man has the incorrigible proclivity of interpreting animal behavior into his own terms.)

Domesticating the cat may indeed be one of man's most admirable and paradoxical accomplishments—encapturing the rapturous moon, the single desire of the unsated human princess. The cat, nevertheless, has only succumbed to man's request in part. This "domestic" cat maintains much of its wild forebears' independence and disinterest in hierarchy. The feline exception, the lion, of course, hunts alone but resides in an established community with a hierarchical system.

Staking out and stalking its prey, the cheetah hunts alone, or in twos.

Unlike domestic dog, who descends from social animals, domestic cat is foreign to man's concept of hierarchy. Cat owners are not likely to consider themselves the masters of their households. Dogs relate to the pack existence and thrive within its confines. The cat, from kittenhood, regards all beings in its path as "fellow cats"—a most undiscriminating approach from this most discriminate of animals. It is this reason that wild cats and domestics respond minimally (or not at all) to training. Circus lions perform with great disdain and even greater distaste for their dubious occupation. Dogs, on the other hand, live to please their human masters. Cats do not perceive humans as masters and do not subscribe to the obedience ritual.

Still, many owners persist that their cat retrieves a ball or sits on command. Unlike canine retrievers, who work for the satisfaction of their master, cats may retrieve a ball because it's fun. You, however, are obligated to continue throwing the ball, taking it from wherever the cat replaces it, and participating only when the cat is willing.

The independence of domestic cats, acquired from the big cats, has been tempered somewhat through cohabitation with man. Man, in his compulsive simplicity, elicits and encourages the cat's childlike

In the Bengal, man has captured only the coat of the leopard cat, leaving this endangered wild feline to thrive in the jungles of Asia. Owner, Gene Johnson, Gogees Cattery.

The Singapura sports a smart, audacious personality, and is quickly adapting to Western ways.

habits and dependence. The ferocity and relentless independence which the cat has gradually foregone through the course of domestication are exchanged for canned cat food, a wool pillow, and a knitted sweater. Additionally the cat inherits a family to call its own, a household of human charges obligated to pay attention to its every whim.

Regardless of how many centuries the felid has shared man's cave, pagoda, or condo, the cat still remains a cat—for this man is grateful and duly smitten, despite himself.

The behavior of domestic cats is keenly akin to their wild counterparts in considering the chase and the hunt. While relatively few cats today find employment as mousers, the chase instincts are still active and affect the house pet's approach to daily life. Stalking a leaf dancing in the wind or a business letter falling off the desk, the cat's physique is instantaneously summoned to concentration. The well-tuned feline possesses the body of a runner and a gymnast, granted an athlete more attuned to a sprint and a quick floor routine than a marathon. Just as the misjudging lion prefers not to chase the antelope that escaped its paw, domestic cats are not keen on much exercise. Kittens, the graceful and momentary exception, will play for hours, too young to appreciate fully the joy of napping between naps.

What a cat is inclined to do and what a cat can do are two very different things. While cats do not opt to run long distances (or even short distances), their bodies are designed for speed and animation. The flexibility of the vertebrae and the subtlety of the collarbone are principally responsible for the cat's uncanny running ability. The placement of the cat's shoulder blades alongside its chest enable the

Never pounce unless you're sure. For felines it's all in the timing.

At three months of age, this blue-point Siamese gets a feel for the grass. Owner, Susan P. Tilton.

joints to travel wider and to lift higher during locomotion. The flexion of the spine, combined with the extension of the shoulder joint, makes it possible for the cheetah to achieve speeds greater than any shoed Arabian, despite its considerably smaller size.

Were it not for domestic cat's diminished chest cavity, cats would be able to endure marathon hauls. As Darwin would have it, cats are, therefore, designed for speed, not endurance, as the construction of their feet indicates. The bones of the cat's feet are thinner and lighter than other similarly sized animals; they are also narrower in diameter and shorter. Unlike hoofed animals, cats do not place

the sole of the foot flat on the ground. The vestigial first toes are higher up on the ankle; the middle two toes are the longest. Locomotion requires only that the ball of the foot is placed on the ground. The evolutionary process has also adjusted the feline's running mechanism through elongation of the metatarsals and the fusion and simplification of the foot bones for strength and the lessening of shock impact.

Perhaps one of the most dramatic similarities between wild and domestic cats arises in the mating ritual. This fascinating aspect will be further probed in the chapter on breeding.

IN THE STILL OF THE DAY

The cat in its domestic state is truly more the sportsman than the hunter. It defines the rules of the chase, schedules "hunting season," and designates the potential game. Without the need to hunt for sustenance, the joy and exigency are in the chase. Cats that are kept as rodent exterminators indeed view their role quite differently than the canine terrier kept for like reasons. The cat's assistance to the farmer is coincidental as opposed to the terrier's aid, which is

It is the lion's perogative to snooze wherever and whenever it chooses—"it's good to be king!"

intentional. Fortunately for farmers, cats like to chase mice, rats, and other scurrying undesirables; for a cat, the chase and perhaps the catch is self-rewarding. Terriers revel in unearthing such varmints because it pleases their masters, not themselves, necessarily.

House cats, domestics who spend 14 to 18 hours asleep daily,

Birds seem less provocative at this height. Tree-climbing household pets experience a change of heart as briskly as the wind blows.

subscribe to an unvoiced reverence for stillness. Indeed their taut and developed musculature enables them to remain absolutely still for an extended duration. The big cats unexceptionally expend many hours static, effectively employing patience as the preferred weapon over running. Likewise, pet cats will pursue anything that violates the necessary state of stillness. The cat's extended state of

Stillness and sleep are venerable to all felines universally. This bicolored Scottish Fold could inspire any British poet or passing metaphysicist. Owner, Susan Stephens.

inactivity, staring unblinkingly with feline foresight, is sacred to the feline family. Sculptors, painters and poets have been long enamored of the cat's concentration: T.S. Eliot refers to the cat's "profound meditation" and persists that: "His mind is engaged in a rapt contemplation . . . of the thought of his . . . ineffable, effable, effanineffable, deep and inscrutable singular name . . . " Not to excavate the feline "effanineffable," the authors rely on the cat's unexplainable, unearthable, unearthly veneration of inactivity.

Driven less by hunger than by a tailed automaton's audacity to transgress the laws of absolute stillness, the cat is obliged to repress the murine delinquent. Natural selection has equipped the cat with specific rodent-catching instincts, although birds, insects and reptiles also violate the stillness. These latter are dealt with less instinctively and often pose less challenge to the pouncing pussy. Bird-hunting felines hunt birds because they move and because they are just fun. The flutter spurred by the fluttering wings and twittering of warbling warblers sends any healthy feline into ear-backed attention. Only the cat's tail treasons the animal's frozen stance, as it twitches at its end, with uncontainable excitement. The pursuit of insects (and an occasional reptile) is a more spontaneous occurence; little forethought is devoted to the instantaneous assailment of a passing beetle or water bug. Claws extended on splayed paws splat the pavement sporadically to suffocate, decapitate, incapacitate, immolate and execute the scoundrel pest—or simply to stop its movement. Smart insects play dead. I once watched a praying mantis, believed to be the wisest of insects, walk through an accelerated rendering of King Lear's death scene upon seeing my spying Shorthair—my cat and I were moved to tears—the mantis was well-read enough to know that cats are exempted from laws protecting its species.

The cat, as the consummate hunter in the animal kingdom, still possesses the inherent tendency to hunt for food. Some cats will

Bird watching is a universal feline pastime. The flutter of the bluejay's wings evokes the twitching tail tip and chat-chattering teeth of this involuntary voyeur behind the glass.

spend hours upon hours chasing, tormenting, killing, and/or eating mice; others won't blink if three blind ones stumble   across their dinner plate. There are various theories explaining all of these behavioral reactions. Kittens begin to unfurl prey-chasing instincts at about three weeks of age. Mothers often can elicit this response from the litter by furnishing live prey. While some barn queens may do this routinely, the authors do not recommend visiting the pet shop to equip the mother with a fresh supply of live prey. Fear not, if mother doesn't encourage the paw-groping of baby mice, this re-

Natural outdoorsmen, cats learn Mother Nature's laws firsthand, with a little tutelage from moms and owners. Maine Coon kitten owned by Sharlyn P. Bass.

Feral felines have proven survival instincts and are accomplished marksmen with their claws and teeth.

sponse can surface later when an enticing rodent wiggles his tail in the cat's direction or simply when the cat is hungry.

The sequence of the hunt takes time for the kitten to learn, usually. Waiting, remaining still and waiting, is the first step; this aspect of the feline's hunting instinct is indicative of the animal's patience and intelligence. Secondly, the cat stalks: crouched close to the grass, the cat gradually approaches the spotted (preferably unexpecting) prey. Muscles contracted in preparation, tail remains flat (though twittering at the tip), the ears back against the head, claws unsheathed, the cat moves with deliberate steps and pounces forward. If successful, the cat seizes its prey with its claws. If the chase must ensue further (i.e., the cat misses) the cat must catch the prey, which requires more energy than the cat prefers to exert. The killing bite, the last instinct acquired, is delivered on the prey's neck, severing the spinal cord and slaying the rodent. Some cats will proceed to eat the catch, others simply will play with the fidgeting carcass,

still others will walk away, pleased with the temporary reinstating of blissful stillness. Behaviorists' studies indicate that many cats do not cross the final killing-bite threshold, and such cats are relegated to toying with or paw-mauling their catch.

Cats in the home, a mouseless home, will do their best to preserve stillness and thus pursue any object that hazards to offend this desired state. Naturally stillness presupposes quiet. The disobedient crumbling of paper or cellophane is cardinal sin number one. Some cat researchers assert that such a sound is reminiscent of prehistoric mice burrowing underground in the wild. There is probably a certain shade of truth to their assertion. Likewise, probing a finger or object in a cardboard box may activate the cat's instinct to grope any peeping rodent's head. Less pseudo-scientific theories rely on the cat's insatiable curiosity and enjoyment of play. The authors are sure that our cats are just diffident of prehistoric rodents and indifferent to behavioral theorists.

*Opposite: All things soft and quiet ensure a peaceable home kingdom. American Curl owned by Caroline Scott. **Below:** Abyssinian preoccupied by munching sounds of giant mice from a past life. Owners of this psychic Aby are Richard and Leslie Gilman. He also reads palms.*

Understanding the cat's mind, the preference for stillness and quiet, is conversant with an appreciation of harmony. In the big ecological picture, the wild cat, on its own, maintains the necessary balance. The ideal habitat is well endowed with shelter and a food source, and one cat. The equilibrium between prey and predator is amply sustained by the cat. The need to reproduce and progenerate the species necessitates socialization and the interruption of solitude.

Below: A Burmese kitten in sable, the "original" breed color. Owner, Herb Zwecker. Opposite: Daring to be different, the Color-point Shorthair exhibits the Siamese conformation with a colorful twist. This blue-eyed blue-lynx-point beauty is owned by Larry Levy.

Pair of Siamese siblings sharing grooming tips. Owner, Phil Morini.

This stumpy-tailed Easterner has done well in making friends in the West. This Japanese Bobtail lives in harmony with owner Janet Bassetti.

'La vie en rose in every key." This bluesy French number is a Chartreaux.

ATONAL HARMONIC SIMPLICITY

In domestic cats, harmony orchestrates their way of life. Defining territories, routines, possessions, charges, etc., is the cat's way of harmonizing with its environment. As peculiar as it sounds, cat is not completely domesticated, not nearly as much so as dog or horse. The idiosyncrasies and behavioral quirks which owners notice and often admire are exemplary of the total lack of adjustment on the cat's part. Providing a well-balanced environment for the cat, including adequate food supply, sleeping quarters, exercise, etc., helps to diminish a cat's unsociability. If reared with care from kittenhood, the adult cat should grow to depend on its human acquaintances and respond affectionately.

In fact, such affection is quite foreign to cats. While big cats in the wild are often portrayed grooming one another, these gestures are geared towards progeneration, the equivalent of flirting and foreplay in humans. Puppies differ from kittens in their immediate re-

Handle with care. Kittens at four weeks of age are fragile and easily frightened; they also exercise less claw discretion. Siamese kittens owned by Marge Naples.

sponse to human handling. Kittens are survivors and do not perceive your groping and/or hugging as essential to survival. Cats still do not acknowledge that humans provide for them; they expect appropriate care and accommodations, as if to say "I didn't ask to be domesticated, so deal with it."

This is not to say that cats (some cats) don't appreciate affection and good care. Many cats are so demonstrative and fondling-oriented that they could almost be dogs (a very high complement to the canine contingency). In the wild, cats learn survival by trusting no one, except themselves; therefore, affection among their own kind is not even usual. To expect a feline to condescend to the likes of humankind and bestow favor, no less affection and familiarity, is predictably boorish and precocious of the reader/owner. As cats continue to share the homes of humankind, it is likely that, with unconditional love and good will, some of the barriers will erode.

However, man must continue to concentrate on "educating" the minds of cats; unfortunately, exhibitors in the cat fancy concern themselves exclusively with outward factors. The obedience training of cats will of course never approach that of dogs but this is more related to cat's lack of cooperation than its lack of intelligence. The self-importance and impervious mental depths of felines, portrayed so well in the depiction of a pensive and confident adult tiger, make training (or convincing) the cat a near-impossible task. It is these authors' opinion that attempting to educate the domestic cat is a medieval notion that will yield no fruit—aren't the cat's individuality and resilience key to our affection for it? Why tamper with perfection?

Cats are a challenge: they are decidedly too complex to understand completely, yet their approach to life is enviably simple; they relay disinterest or abomination with half a glance, yet continue to

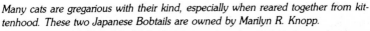

Many cats are gregarious with their kind, especially when reared together from kittenhood. These two Japanese Bobtails are owned by Marilyn R. Knopp.

purr; their keen survival instincts substantiate their high intelligence, yet they refuse to acknowledge the most elementary command.

Canine buffs too quickly conclude that cats are simply dumb, as they point to their obedience-trained retriever playing dead on the carpet. Feline advocates take for granted that a cat is too smart to roll on its back and look inane to amuse a mere human. Dogs are repulsively pedestrian, in the feline guise, and allow humans too much control. The inherent discretion of each feline is crucial to the survival of the race; the individuality of the cat and its void of pack instincts verify the cat's (self-determined) superiority over other domestic animals.

"Baggage," a white domestic shorthair, enjoys the company of many well-meaning Husky buddies at the kennel of James and Maureen Kent.

An impatient and plebian romp through Queen Anne's lace and impatiens—a young blue and white bicolor American Curl traipsing through a floral field.

Yet cats are committed to understanding mankind and attempt to communicate in active ways. It is not unusual for the family cat to show interest in the daily goings-on, or at least feign interest. That cats are curious goes without saying. A kitten's absolute awe of the world around it does not astound its new owner, for (sadly) most of us consider the morning chatter of birds, the movement of the trees, and the shadow of the sun pretty matter-of-fact occurrences.

Observing the human antics of owner Geraldine V. Cox, a reticent Chartreaux keeps a secret well.

While catwatching is an unspoken affinity of many people, peoplewatching is an even more amusing pastime, for cats, that is. We humans are all too quick to laugh at how peoplelike our cats can be. These sophisticated little fur people wittingly absorb human tendencies and habits. Many female cats spread their hinds in embarassingly unladylike fashion, others may sleep or eat with peculiar though familiar (or familial) charm. Cats assuredly understand more about humans than we do about them, though they publish considerably fewer books.

Above: Two well-shelved British Shorthairs communicate the biped carryings-on they've witnessed. *Below:* Wise and timeless, the Persian has shared domestic life with man for centuries.

DECODING "MORRIS"

Repeatedly man has interpreted feline language to decode its meaning; while his success may vary, his sincerity is always admirable. We join the ranks of erroneous and redundant humankind to enumerate and interpret our favorite feline gestures, phrases and fetishes.

In the creation of new breeds, permutations and mutations of color and coat, man experiences like variations in the feline personality and adaptability. A unique and affectionate Oriental Shorthair owned by Rita Albert.

Purring is an exclusive function of felines, most felines. The bobcat is the only one of the world's cats that does not share in the family treasure. The origination of purring in the cat's body has been explained variously through the centuries. Many curious and charming legends mystify its genesis. Today scientists purport a different, surely less imaginative, hypothesis to explain the phenomenon. The cat's false vocal cords, the two membranous folds behind

Purring is indulgent, involuntary and in and out and . . .

Active in mind and body, the Exotic Shorthair never conceals the fact that it is plotting. The personality of the breed reflects the temperaments of both its ancestors, the Persian and the American Shorthair. Owner, Elita Cooper MacNeil.

the larnyx, vibrate to produce the purr. Domestic cats are capable of purring while inhaling and exhaling, while the wild cats can only purr during inhalation. Just as cat's voices vary in tonality, volume, and employment, purrs can vary similarly. Some cats purr constantly, others purr only rarely. It is likely that less frequent purrers tend towards unsociability and unwelcome guests. Traditionally, purring has been viewed as an indication of the cat's contentment, but actually cats may purr to communicate their willingness or even desire for human attention or intervention. Sick cats may purr to voice their need for your care. Incidentally, the first use of the purr in the feline repertoire is to indicate to littermates that feeding time has commenced.

Another common cat vocalization is the growl. Domestic cats and wild cats share this sometimes less-than-subtle indicator that they are not amused and are prepared to strike. Kittens are taught by their mothers to growl as queens often growl to attract the litter's usually divided attention.

Growling is often succeeded by hissing and spitting, felinity's most unfailing and gauche social faux pas, and the response to an unmistakable threat. All cats hiss and spit. Even the puma, the only wild cat unable to roar, is able to muster quite an impressive display of teeth, saliva, and a punctuating *sss*.

There is much undercurrent concerning the origin of the cat's hiss; assumedly it is a means of protective mimicry on the cat's part. The snake also hisses and also spits, and usually convinces its frightened and damp confronter to retreat. The cat allegedly mimics the snake's proven, venom-promising approach by hissing, spitting,

Mother is chiefly responsible for the kitten's proper elocution and usage of the feline vocabulary. Meow lesson underway with Colorpoint Shorthair and Siamese youngster. Owner, Alice Angermeyer.

A distinct advantage of being able to spit!

Effective as they are dramatic, the cat's defense mechanisms assume possession of the fearless and/or frightened feline—fur on end, claws unsheathed and a convincing ophidian hiss.

slicking back its ears (to give its head a more serpentine flair), and switching its tail—hoping its halfbrained assailant is mousy and imperceptive enough to flee and not notice its fur or fleas.

While the authors could never impugn the craftiness or industry of the feline species, there are certain factors to consider. Not all snakes are venemous; not all snakes hiss; and very few venomous snakes hiss. There are zoos and greenhouses full of legitimate ex-

Too much pseudo-biology can be tiresome to even the most attentive feline.

amples of species that employ mimicry for protection or reproduction purposes: the non-venomous king snake coyly impersonating the deadly coral snake; the very edible viceroy butterfly mimicking the bigger and bitter-tasting monarch butterfly; certain orchid's genitals impersonating certain female wasps (to attract male wasps for pollen); and the sacrilegiously crafty praying mantis preying on unsuspecting insects by impersonating an orchid (not to be confused with the already mimicking, aforementioned imposter orchid, of course). Cats parroting or aping snakes, however, is a bit farfetched. Instead of padding feline behavior with human rationalization, as we of the accused species tend to do, we can simply ascertain that the cat spits because it can. Admittedly this takes the zing out of the cat's hiss, but surely not its "venom."

"Meow" honks a Tonk. The Tonkinese discourses with the most eloquent of cats—people talk is second nature to many cats. Owners, Sheila and Martha Reams.

Meow, mew, murmur, murmur: The most common of all cat calls is the meow. This is equivalent to the canine bark and is arguably less annoying in large dosages. Nevertheless, an atonal mass of mewing, squealing, and crying feral felines (probably toms) vocalizing on a mid-summer night, irreverent to the moon, promises to be nightmarish. The mew is the cat's most active form of communication; it can indicate a wanting to eat, to drink, to leave; it may simply help dissolve boredom or loneliness; it may mean nothing at all (and why should it?). Kittens mew from a very young age and rely on it for mom's attention.

The utterance properly pronounced contains no less than three syllables: *mi-a:ou*. Most adult cats are capable of enunciating all

"Mew" too!

three syllables and the acceptable variants of the word; kittens need proper rearing to get beyond the insufferable *mhrn*, which is too enthusiastic and shreddingly high-pitched (Caballé on a bad day, perhaps). A minority faction in Shropshire favors a two-syllable pronunciation, excluding the last one, making for a simple *mi-a, mi-a*. These open-mouthed, tongue-wagging feral extremists need more traditional breeding (i.e., upbringing). True cats, however, subscribe to the three-syllable school, properly stressing the middle *a* syllable. It is worthy of mention that a trend in Boston-proper recently began emphasizing the last *ou* syllable (presumably in response to the Shropshire clan), some even repeated the *ou*.

During the mating process, however, the queen's rendering of *mi-a:ou* inevitably changes to more of a *mmMMEEHKXCHOOWR-R8RREE–OOUOUOUou* frenetically, not phonetically, as any given number of variants and syllables is acceptable since the mating ritual is exempted from daily feline etiquette. The chapter on breeding in this book will discuss this ineffable, unspellable utterance in more detail.

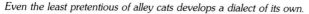

Even the least pretentious of alley cats develops a dialect of its own.

A felicitous feline smile and a hearty "hello" communicate fondness from this Japanese Bobtail. The partially tailed and tailless breeds cannot depend too profusely on that absent apparatus to express themselves. Owner, Janet Bassetti.

Beyond these telling vocal aerobics, most felines have very expressive tails—that is, those felines who have tails have very expressive ones. The Manx, Japanese Bobtail, Cymric, and American Bobtail are the family's four tailless cats. In tailed cats, this fairly lengthy apparatus is essentially a barometer of the animal's decision-making process, if cats do indeed make decisions. Cats' tails wag or twitch when they are excited and faced with prospective ambivalence: "Should I go out, or shouldn't I?"; "Should I bite the moron's hand that's pulling my ear, or shouldn't I?"; "Should I

Taillessness does not help the cat with balance, although the lack of that twitching apparatus is a distinct advantage in bird-napping on the lawn. Japanese Bobtail owned by Marilyn Knopp.

claw the new waterbed or should I sleep?''; ''Should I eat that mouse or just mangle it for a while?''; etc. All of these conflicts in the cat's head are tapped out by its tail.

Tail wagging is also instrumental in the feline balancing act. Its one-foot-at-a-time walking pattern along a ledge, fence, or railing may occasionally need a tilt to the right or left, and the tail does this adeptly. Tail wagging, however, is not instrumental to the pursuit of birds on the front lawn, unless you don't mow too often and the cat can hide its twitching tail tip.

Feline body language, like people body language, is an important mode of communication. Cats in the mood are quite expressive with their owners and are disposed to relay their intentions. A cat rolling over on its belly when you enter the room is a subtle, though evocative, statement to its human charge. This delightfully D.H. Lawrence gesture opens up the cat's vulnerability and is a sure indication of the cat's trust. A similar, though more energetic, gesture

Above: *The Russian Blue swooshes its tail to indicate its delight. This lip-smacking comrade is owned by Lucille Westbrook.* **Below:** *The full-brush tail of the Somali wags contentedly for visitors, especially the Fuller Brush salesman. Owner, Abby C.A. Carbine.*

would be the cat's rubbing itself against your legs. This friendly exchange is as everyday as "hello" or "good morning," yet never broaches the cliche level of our mundane matinal salutations. Additionally, cats are very partial to scent-gland exchanges, recognizing friends and foes by their scents; rubbing against your legs is a mutual exchange of cordial smells.

Understanding the cat—its language, moods, and instincts—is vital in our roles as good owners. One non-cat-owning babysitter once sat at my home, not budging from my couch for four hours—absolutely petrified, fearful of her slightest movement—while my "threatening" six-month-old, blue-eyed Angora purred loudly, enjoying her new friend's company. This true story illustrates how much for granted we take our cat's communicative processes, i.e., any fool can tell a blissful purr from a growl, or can they?? Even so,

A trusting silver tabby displays its belly for owner Carol Rothfeld.

Not just any human can embrace a cat with open arms. This happy Singapura belongs to Tord and Suzanne Svenson.

not everyone is cut out to be a cat owner; the sensitivity and good-humored tolerance required are special traits which only true cat people exhibit.

Are you one such person? —read on, O brave fancier . . . . . .

Left: Pair of camping Balinese in pink puffy tent. Owners, Paulette and Frank Dentremont. *Below:* One white Cymric kitten gift-wrapped to go. Owner, Vickie L. Hansen.

Winnowing & Window Shopping

Most avid cat fanciers will attest that an owner doesn't really pick his cat, but rather that the cat picks his owner. Visiting a litter of wriggling and furry, tail-twitching kittens (pardon us, Sphinx and Manx people, respectively) and eyeing the one for you may indeed be a matter of the approving kitten simply winking to cue you on. Of course there are always general considerations: some only prefer longhaired cats, others short; some despise white cats and fawn over tabbies; some prefer fur, others not; some like long tails, others none at all.

The tremendous king-sized ears and silky coat of the Cornish Rex make it the choice of many cat lovers.

Ginger is a genuine preference, as are big ears, blunt noses, nosy expressions, blue eyes, green eyes, blue and green eyes, blue-green eyes. As many cats and colors and hues that exist, there are human preferences . . . in fact, human preference is the primary source of creation and interference in the feline universe.

The concept of cat breeds is inspired by man, sustained by man, and tolerated by felines (or most felines). Felines, more so than canines, have been both resilient and resistant to the tinkering of man. The anatomical structure of the cat remains essentially the same from breed to breed, essentially. Relative to domestic dog, domestic cat's conformation dissensions are subtle at best. The domestic cat world cannot compete with the classic canine comparison: Great

Opposite: The select companion of royalty for centuries, the Siamese continues to enrapture fanciers. This is the first male cinnamon-lynx-point Siamese cat in the U.S., considered by some registries a Colorpoint Shorthair. Owner, Linda and Elaine Kochis. *Above:* The American Shorthair personifies everyone's expectations of a "regular" cat—sturdy, personable, and simply attractive. Owner, Terry Havel.

Dane is to Chihuahua . . . Maine Coon is to ?? Nevertheless, we are fortunate that breeders have not tried to attain such divergence, since the output likely would yield horrifying results.

Historically, the cat has changed only minimally. Etchings and renderings of cats in the ancient arts of Egypt depict animals that look surprisingly similar to our domestic cats today. Instead of fanciers' clawing at each other to prove that *their* breed is the actual cat depicted on the tomb wall, together cat people should celebrate the soundness (and near-perfection) of the feline "indestructible automaton," as Ambrose Bierce phrased it.

The Egyptian Mau, preserved in a silver coat, is an efficient and resourceful purebred cat. Owner, Andre Jeannotte.

FIT, FITTER, FITTEST

Untamed relations in the rough, hacking guns and shrinking forests; domestics surviving in a cement society; intermeddling men peer unwittingly to determine the destiny of the world's felines. That the world is over-populated with domestic cats is a common fact. Not since the fourteenth century has there been a shortage of cats for man's needs. In the United States alone, nearly eight million cats are euthanized annually. Only about one-third of the cats adopted are actually kept for the duration of their lives. These statistics, as reported in 1989 by the Humane Society of the United States, speak to potential cat owners and cat-owning cat lovers alike.

The decision to spay or neuter your cat is a simple one. If you do not plan to breed the cat, have it sterilized. Freeing the cat of sexual hang-ups and frustrations, which plague mankind so regularly, is indeed a service; not contributing to the gross over-population of felines, however, is truly the virtue intended.

A contraceptive pill is available for the modern queen who is not ready to begin her family. Abuse of this device has resulted in negative side effects, as well as the greater potential of uterine disease. A veterinarian's counsel is advised for owners who wish to investigate this path. Most vets are willing to discuss the prospects of contraceptives and will keep such inquiries confidential, so that the worldly feline involved (and her owner) does not acquire a reputation.

Man must accept the responsibility for the over-population of domestic felines. Consider that wild cats cycle only once per annum while domestic cats go in "heat" three times per annum. Man in the process of domesticating the "king of the jungle" accidentally forged two more yearly cycles, potentially producing three times as many cats than would have otherwise been created, per female, per year. Male domestics, like male wilds, like male practically anything, are instinctually pro-progenerating on a regular basis. Man must as-

An unwanted litter of even the finest purebreds will be a heartbreaking occurrence. Breeders and fanciers must secure homes for litters before planning a mating. This blue-eye basketful includes both Siamese and Colorpoint Shorthairs. Owner, Irene B. Brounstein.

sume an aptly responsible role in this world of "too many cats."

Yet this is not to purport that *every* human should own a cat, or is deserving of such proprietorship. Since only one-third of the cats adopted from shelters actually remain in those owners' homes for the duration of their lives, apparently not everyone has fully explored the realm of cat ownership and understood the responsibilities involved.

Certain cat facts, obvious though they be, need to be *italicized*. Kittens, almost without exception, grow into cats (reportedly, some

No matter how hypnotic the stare of a stray kitty, the decision to adopt a cat must be approached realistically and intelligently. American Shorthair, owned by Carol Rothfeld.

While not the proper way to handle such a young kitten, the trust and love evident in the eyes of this Exotic Shorthair are remarkable. Owner, Elita Cooper MacNeil.

kittens grow into dogs, but the authors have less than sufficient data to support these very rare cases). Kittens and young cats have an appeal all their own and may entice the less-than-worthy cat admirer into committing to ownership. And secondly, cats live considerably long lives. Fifteen to 20 years would be considered an average lifespan for a domestic cat. Two British tabbies reportedly lived to 34 and 36 years of age. Ownership surely is a commitment worth considerable forethought, to avoid regret-filled afterthoughts. Where will I be in ten years and is there a place for my cat?

The legality of owning a cat is usually considered simpler than owning a dog. Most landlords allow cats in their dwellings, but it is necessary to investigate this matter. Be sure to read your rental agreement thoroughly. Harboring a stowaway stray day after day soon becomes a nuisance. If your landlord is not hostile towards felines, he may be willing to listen to your request. Some landlords compromise by appending a pet-owner's fee to the monthly check.

Left: Birman kittens in a very domestic setting. These kitchen-counter babies belong to Betty A. Cowles.
Below: Chestnut Oriental Shorthair, owned by Irene B. Brounstein.

THE CAT IN THE HOUSE

Owner responsibility begins before actual ownership. Potential cat owners must evaluate their reasons for wanting a cat, the time they have to dedicate to a cat, and the kind of cat they desire. For centu-

Bengal kittens can fit well into any house. Owner, Michael E. Nelson.

ries cats have provided man with the simple pleasure of companionship. While man continually tries to put his finger on the meaning of life and living, cat has rested on his lap, or shoulder, or fidgeting brow to assure him that he will never know. (Smug and exclusive, felines effectively have kept such answers to themselves.) Man's reasons for wanting a cat haven't changed too much over the generations. Men have on occasion shackled the cat to join their forces and work, but this is scarcely the reason man chooses cat as his companion in the twentieth century. Cats have successfully resisted man's pleas to help him complete his daily chores, save the

The American Curl was developed from a mutation in ear shape found in farm cats in the U.S. This black Curl is owned by Anne Wilson.

The Siamese breeds have proven to be among the most adaptable and tolerant of cats. Colorpoint Shorthair owned by Nicole Ledoux.

working cat population that mouses in barns for farmers, leaving the herding and guarding and hunting and digging and pulling and fighting and finding to the dogs and other suitably benign, obligingly burdened beasts. The cheetah has proven the one feline fluke, as it has been employed effectively at man's side as a big-game hunter; man's appreciation of the animal's compliance is rendered hypocritical as his shoulder turns and he hunts his side-cat with his own firearms. While cats have never and will never perform any mundane canine function, man still deems it necessary to have a cat by his side. The less-fondled felines, the barn cats and yard cats, are unique in that they work for their daily fish—and perhaps expect less of their human charges. Our semi-righteous house-dwelling felines expect a plentitude of attention, respect, and care, and are not likely to be as exalted as their humble cousins on Judgment Day.

An owner must decide that he has the time to devote to a feline housemate. While cats require considerably less accommodation than their canine counterparts and some other potential pets, they still make certain demands on the owner. An owner must be aware of these demands and be willing to oblige the cat's intercession.

It is vital to regard the entire household when considering the acquisition of a cat. Everyone in the house should be taken into consideration and should want the new cat to become a part of his/her life. Children and dogs, adults' charges, deserve particular attention. Young children often relate to the new kitten as they would their rattle or ragdoll, hitting and grabbing at it with no concern for its well being. This behavior is not cruel, that is intentionally cruel, though the effect on the badgered Balinese or Ragdoll is the same. Children must be taught to treat the cat with the respect due it and to regard it as a living thing, not a replica stuffed with shavings. Although cats do not suck the breath out of infants, as one misguided anti-feline school once asserted, they can suffocate a child by lying on its face. Cats should be kept out of nurseries for the child's sake.

Kittens may or may not be allured by tropical fish. This soon-to-be-editor of Tropical Fish Hobbyist *magazine is a young Somali.*

Candid and mutually dependent, this dog and cat duo regularly pals around.

Cats are not ill-meaning but actually enjoy the company and warmth of the child. Felines are inclined to face-to-face contact; many cats seek out and "kiss" their owner's face.

Dogs are also a consideration. Some breeds of dog are more accepting of felines. The rule of paw here is to raise the animals together from a young age. If a household has an adult dog, opting for an adult cat may be wise, since an older cat can protect itself better than a kitten. Do not assume that big dogs don't like cats and small dogs do. Many great big dogs, such as Great Danes and Great Pyrenees, love cats while some less-great small dogs have notable distaste for felines (the Maltese and Pekingese are potential culprits). Ideally, properly acclimated dogs and cats should be able to share a household with few problems and the classic simile "fighting like cats and dogs" is both cliché and untrue.

FELID ATTRACTION

The convinced and willing potential owner now must decide what kind of cat he desires or deserves. In the purebred cat world, there are three basic types available for purchase: pet type, breeder stock

The Japanese Bobtail is a clean, responsive cat with a growing fancy. Owner, M. R. Knopp.

and show specimen. The least expensive and most accessible of these types is fortunately the most popular: pet-type cats are those animals who are desired by owners who do not have intentions of breeding or showing them. Persons who wish to enter the purebred world as a breeder should purchase an animal of proven, pedigreed lineage, registered by the appropriate body. Potential participants in exhibition should purchase show-quality animals, registered cats

A cat as stunning and demanding as the Persian "won't be ignored." Owner, Geri Hamilton.

who demonstrate the possibility of adhering closely to the standard of perfection.

Pet cats are the only ones that come without registration papers and without "all their parts." Both breeder-stock cats and show cats require papers and unaltered "parts." A breeder cat queen is capable of producing countless show-quality offspring, though she may not be show-quality herself; the quality is in the genes!

Opposite: The Maine Coon, a native American purebred, stands out among the hardiest of the longhaired breeds. Owners, Lyman and Elena Stewart. **Above:** This champion Longhair boasts a colorful history of show-ring successes.

The owner's preference plays the most important part in choosing the sex of the new cat, and of course choosing the breed. The former considerations become quite irrelevant if one is opting for simply a purebred pet, as an "it" burns paper, scissors and rock—and pedigrees too. Otherwise, the choice of male or female relies on the owner's decision. Owners desiring a breeder cat probably desire a female so that they can have the experience of the litter at home, as well as the kittens to sell or keep. The temperament and disposition of the male is often different than the female. Males generally are more outgoing and uninhibited; females tend towards more shy and reserved. While the male grows larger than the female, size is rarely a point in question.

Regardless of how impeccably one plans his purchase of a new cat, serendipity sometimes provides the most rewarding acquisition; many owners have been adopted by a stray while in the process of making the decision upon the "right" cat. While every stray that wanders into your yard may not be the prodigal, perfect pet, many owners have acquired their most loved feline companions in this way. This alleviates so many of these oftimes-difficult decisions.

While many cat advisors recommend that the new owner purchase a kitten as opposed to an adult cat, there are a number of worthwhile considerations. Generally, cats are less work than kittens, require less discipline (unless they were previously owned by

An individual's situation will dictate the choice of a kitten or an adult; the choice between the two sexes is but a matter of individual preference. Bombay, owned by Herb Zwecker.

The adult Maine Coon requires a considerable amount of grooming, although the Coon is a clean and self-sufficient cat. Owner, Connie Webb.

uncouths), and are less actively inquisitive. Kittens, especially if very young, require nearly constant attention and care. They are of course more malleable and easier to teach right from wrong. Adult cats may be set in their ways and, regardless of your reasoning or ruling, their ways are the only ways. Some persons opt for an adult cat if they have young children in the household. Kittens tend to be

Littermates often make congenial companions for one another. Persons considering the adoption of two cats might wish to acquire a handsome pair of Maine Coons like this one.

hugged and/or mauled by very young tots. Nonetheless, both kittens and adults make wonderful pets if properly reared and treated with care and genuineness.

The decision to own one or two cats is an important one. The authors recommend that everyone own at least two felines. Especially if an owner has his heart set on a particular exotic purebred, a "regular" cat invited to share in the home is a positive way of curbing the feline over-population. Incidentally, it should be mentioned to any exuberant, excessive cat lover out there that there are laws concerning the number of cats one household is permitted to keep. Doing your part by adopting three dozen strays each month may not be well received by the board of health, your neighbors, your spouse, and/or your dog.

Above: The Abyssinian has swept the popularity polls like the desert winds. These well-balanced, beautiful shorthairs have growing fancies in America and Europe. Blue Abyssinian owned by Sheila Dentico. **Below:** The Himalayan or Colorpoint Persian (Longhair) is a personable but proud breed of longhaired cat. For the person requiring a dedicated feline housemate, the Himalayan cannot be overlooked. Owner, Anne Wilson.

WHICH PREFERRED PERFECTION?

The selectivity of purebred cat progeneration, the maintenance and advancement of breeds, is in harmony with the house rules of Mother Nature. Just as all the local felines of Burma eventually acquired similar features—a breed, if you will—man has established a few dozen breeds of domestic cat. Felids in the wild, too, are selective and will not reproduce with any tom, tom, or tom that comes

Above: Selective breeding has produced such glamorous felines as the Ragdoll. The wonderous Ragdoll always has blue eyes and may or may not have the trademark (trademarked ®) white mittens. Owner, Linda Swierczynski. **Opposite:** The Color-point Shorthair can be distinguished from the Siamese by its dilute lynx markings. Owner, Larry Levy.

along. Responsible breeders work toward the betterment of their cats and do not subscribe to tinkering mindlessly with various breeds for "new joyous creations."

With the denaries of cat breeds already firmly established, and the hundreds of colors available therein, the creation of new breeds seems regretfully frivolous. While certain owners may claim that Si-

amese cats, for instance, provide more quality companionship than any other purebred cat (or any other cat), the truth is that any cat, properly reared, socialized and cared for, is capable of providing optimum companionship for its owner. Nevertheless, it is not the authors' intention to reprimand the creators of new breeds, nor to curtail the development of new purebred cats. Boasting an attestable appreciation for beauty, cat fanciers are a demanding and discriminate lot who need variation and stimulation to survive, like cats themselves, we suppose.

The semi-exclusive fraternity that owns purebred cats is expanding day by day. The United States, as the melting pot of the world's races, has found it particularly in vogue to own a purebred cat. The American nation has no natives (even the Indians had to trek here so many moons ago), and as such, it is comprised of mixed breeds or ethnic-Americans. Italian-Americans, Polish-Americans, British-Americans, Irish-Americans, etc.—Americans each hold on to their individual roots. It is somehow fitting that these "natives" should opt to own not just any "mutt" cat, but a purebred, a pedigree, a

"Judge, smudge! I feel svelte, svelte, svelte." A wonderfully tubular Oriental Shorthair owned by Lisa Greco being examined in the ring.

Scottish Americans and Scotsmen alike take pride in their kilt-wearing felid, the Scottish Fold. Owners, Gayle Rasmussen and June Young.

distinctive feline. Ethnically proud Americans then quest for a cat of a similarly pure origin. No small amount of yuppie pride and authenticity accompanies an affected yawn: "Yes, yes, this is a *purebred* Abyssinian." Of course America is not exclusive to this mindset—British and Canadian cat lovers take tremendous pride in purebred cats and smile most winningly on native Brit or Canadian felids, without sparing teeth or dimples. Surely Great Britain has preserved and promoted more purebred domestic animals than any other nation.

Choosing the breed of cat for you is an exciting and mind-opening undertaking. Over forty breeds of domestic cat exist for the potential owner to choose from. While size is hardly a consideration in choosing a breed, coat length, personality, and tendencies are each to be addressed. Cat breeds vary from the sleekest, tightest coat to the long, exuberant coat (to no coat at all). Breed personalities vary considerably; some breeds such as the Siamese and Burmese are extroverted and fun-loving, while others, such as the Himalayan and Chartreux, are serious and pensive, not given to excessive frolicking. Other breeds are more vocal and energetic; others are quiet and insouciant. Perhaps the most substantial consideration is the appeal of the breed to the eye. Regardless of a breed's personality, if a potential owner doesn't find the look and aura of the breed enticing, its personality will hardly have a chance to bloom. A fancier may indeed like the warm-hearted temperament of the Sphynx but become alarmed by its shocking appearance; incidentally, it is not so rare for a cat to win over its unenamored new owner within 24 hours or less. It is true, also, that not all members of a given breed adhere directly to the personality de-

Opposite: *The Sphynx is the only established breed of hairless cat. It was developed by Canadian breeders in the late 1960s.*
Above: *The British Shorthair, a strong and resilient cat native to England, is somewhat smaller than the American rendition of the domestic shorthair, the American Shorthair. Both breeds come in all colors imaginable. This blue belongs to Marcella and Ronald Syminiuk.* ***Below:*** *Two more blue beauties, these are long-coated Russian Blues, known as Nebelungs. This sophisticated experimental breed offers all of the charm of the Blue in a long, single coat. Owner, Cora Cobb.*

scribed in the standard. More so than with any other pet, the cat is an individual through and through and may not be given to the chicanery or aloofness which is expected of its breed—one more reason for loving cats.

Green-eyed silver tabby American Shorthair. This all-American cat distributes affection evenly to all members of its human family. As a breed, the American Shorthair also favors the company of other felines.

Since this book also discusses the various types of wild cats, it is only appropriate that the authors address the potential of owning a wild cat as a pet. Generally speaking, ocelots and margays are the most commonly kept wild cats. Ownership of such animals is warted by negative facts, no less the actual acquisition of a lion or cougar, which is illegal, incidentally, practically everywhere. Initially it is necessary to learn what local or state ordinances pertain to the ownership of a wild cat. Most areas, if they permit ownership, require permits and a tedium of other regulatory forms. It is difficult to acquire these animals and their scarce numbers in the wild

All the allure and beauty of the wild in a domestic package: the Bengal.

should be enough to thwart even the greatly enamored. Having to declaw and defang these animals just to keep them as pets adds further distaste to ownership. The authors greatly favor both the ocelot and margay, as well as the other wild felids discussed in this book. However we cannot encourage the ownership of any one of them since it is detrimental to the cats and often harmful to the humans involved. Zoos, while not favored by some, have far more adequate accommodations for these animals; if you love the ocelot and margay, you will visit them in zoos—as we do!

Ocelots weigh about 29 pounds and have been kept as pets by civilians. Fortunately this frowned-upon practice has waned today; unfortunately so have the ocelot's numbers.

BOBBING   RETAILERS' TALL TALES

Certain breeds, less familiar and more difficult to breed, cannot be found at pet shops. Cornish Rex, owned by Catherine Lachenmayer.

There are three potential sources from which to acquire a cat: a local pet shop, a cat breeder, and an animal shelter. Each of these sources can be reliable ones for the right cat. Since a pet shop is not able to stock every breed of cat in every possible color, breeders become a valuable source to cat owners. Pet shops can help potential owners locate reputable breeders of cats which they do not have available. For the person looking for a "regular" cat, that is a mixed-breed or stray, an animal shelter is a sound choice since the cats often come neutered and vaccinated.

If you require a show-quality or breeder-quality purebred cat, a breeder may be your only option. Pet shops carry a variety of purebred cats but these are intended mostly for existences as exquisite house cats. The prices charged at pets shops are generally less than what a breeder will charge you for his best cats. Remember that breeders want to see their cats with the most potential enter the show ring or breeding forum in order for their reputations as breeders to grow and improve. There is very little rationale for them to allow their champion of champions to mill around your home looking pretty and turning only the heads of your visitors. The rule of thumb here, undeniably, is *beware!* Never be afraid to ask questions of the seller. He should be able to provide the answers as well as the documentation (pedigree and sales papers). There are quack-breeders and quack pet-shops (and bad animal shelters too). Do not settle for second best—if the seller cannot meet your standards, move on to another.

Japanese Bobtail kittens maneuvering their escape. Owner-warden, Janet Bassetti.

Upon locating the animal or litter of your choice, inspect the individual(s) carefully. The coats should be resilient and healthy looking; the eye should be clear and the eyelids free of scales. Bare spots on the coat may indicate ringworm. Noses can be wet and cold, but not runny. Signs of diarrhea should be sought out. The animal should be alert and zesty. Consider the size and weight for the kitten's age. Hearing and vision can be checked by crumpling paper, rattling keys, or simply moving and talking to the cat.

If all the cats meet these criteria of health, then choose the one which appeals to your eye and taste. Colors may vary as will patterns; kitten coats may get darker or lighter as they grow up.

The most ideal way to carry home your latest acquisition is in a carrying case. These are available in different sizes, styles, colors,

*Below: Prospective owners should learn the vital signs of a healthy kitten: shiny coat, clear eyes and nose, alertness. Maine Coon kitten. **Opposite:** Let me bend your ear about a spectacular new breed, the bended-eared American Curl. In addition to the endearing personality of the Curl breed, its ears surely add to its charms. Owners, Michael Tucker and Caroline Scott.*

Among the longhaired cat breeds, the Birman stands out for its exceptional coloration, appearing in all four Siamese points, and all-occasion white gloves. Owner, Betty A. Cowles.

Right: For purposes of travel and exhibition, accustoming the cat to a crate proves expeditious. *Below:* Members of a breed should resemble one another in every possible way. Siamese, owned by Phil Morini.

etc., at most pet shops or pet supply outlets. It is wise to acquire one as soon as possible since it is necessary for trips to the veterinarian, boarding house, show ring, etc. If you do not have time to purchase a cat case before the cat, use a terry-cloth towel to carry the cat. This makes it easy to hold the cat and will protect you from its frightened frightful claws. Make the cat feel secure in your arms, be gentle and talk softly, as this is the beginning of a life shared together.

Above: Providing tasteful accommodations presents a challenge to every owner. The Cymric, the longhaired version of the Manx, requires a sensible owner. Owner, Vickie L. Hansen. *Below:* Trio of Norwegian Forest kittens owned by Pat Andrews. *Opposite:* Dilutes and pastels—the Javanese blends into any home or background. A long coat and plume tail differentiate the breed from the Siamese and Colorpoint Shorthair. Owner, Karen Christmann.

Catering & Care

The requests and longings of our feline housemates instinctively make our agenda. However, that the cat's open-air kin enjoy the seclusion and warmth of tree hollows and caves and the romance and freedom of a decipherable sky does not mandate that every potential cat owner need assemble do-it-yourself caverns and skylights nor cultivate indoor wildernesses. Comparatively speaking, catering to a domestic cat requires little expense, though much taste.

Providing the cat with an acceptable and appreciably lavish indoor life depends on the proper home setting. "Cats have felines too" as one cartoon artist once cast for copy. Cats perceive and respond well to their environment. Bringing a young kitten home for the first time to a barren apartment or, conversely, to a home filled with well-dusted untouchables is both an unfair and poorly considered first step toward responsible cat ownership. More appropriately, the cat should be able to move freely through most of the home area, without a hyperanxious owner fretting an unguided paw and without dangerous objects and crevices impeding every step. Kittens, in particular, need consistent but discriminate supervision. Additionally, the cat should have adequate seclusion for retiring.

Necessary indoor accommodations for the cat include a feeding dish and water bowl, sanitation box and litter, scratching post and bed. Cats, as unanimously gracious creatures, often accept only the former accommodations, frequently spurning the post and bed, deeming them superfluous and/or vile. Rightly, many owners, seasoned and green, complain that their cat does not use its scratching post and persists in clawing everything but and/or that their cat has never slept (and will never sleep) in any bed intentionally provided for that purpose. While certain incentive-building measures can be

Nature does well to accommodate the jungle and forest cats. Aloof and proud, lions make their beds on the rocky heights, overseeing their kingly province.

taken, some cats are simply unconvinced, regardless of how impeccably constructed, pretty, or pleasant smelling the petshop item is.

Regarding scratching posts, many writers and researchers have voiced their suppositions. Some believe that the cat chooses the object that it will claw based primarily upon the scent of the object. Very often, the preferred scent is that of the cat's preferred person, often the feeder and provider. One owner, whose cat preferred, above everyone else, the neighbor, reported that after a visit from

Outdoor accommodations for the indoor cat are minimal to non-existent. This rock-gardening Birman kitten poses patiently for photographer Robert Pearcy.

the neighbor the cat invariably chose as a claw-grooming object the seat cushion on which the neighbor sat. However, not all owners experience similar behavior, and indeed not all researchers agree that scent is the object's appeal. Others believe that cats choose their claw-honing object based on its texture, and that most cats have a preferred material. Still other researchers maintain that contributing tactile and olfactory preferences to the cat's choice of the object is not giving the feline nature its due: cats claw what they claw because they wish to claw what they claw, no buts about it. No finding on the cat's use of a scratching post is conclusive, however. The authors believe that likely each has some degree of truth and validity, and that the degree can vary from individual cat to individual cat. Most likely all three factors play a part in the cat's choice of a scratching post.

As a scratching post that is actually scratched can save both furni-

Above: *"Kitty" claims her bed. Domestic shorthair owned by Barbara Johnson.*
Below: *Maintenance of the claws requires an indoor post or nearby tree. This well-fed tom hones its claws while marking its territory.*

Dripping faucets and cool stainless steel entertain this blue British Shorthair. Before a cat can feel comfy in your home, it will likely have to sit and/or sleep in every place dreamable. Owners, Marcella and Ronald Syminiuk.

ture and frustration, it is recommended that the owner purchase or construct such a device. If the cat shows no interest in the post and persists in clawing other objects, then the owner can try covering the post with a scented replica of the material that the cat most commonly scratches. If this too fails, then perhaps either the material or the scent was the wrong choice, and after additional consideration an alternative can be tried—not to take offense if the scent was your own, for these findings are truly proposals and not conclusions.

Cats "make their own bed," and in no bed that any cat has made has it ever hesitated to sleep. Unlike dogs, cats do not need (and may not want) the owner to clear a corner and insert a bed, place the cat in the bed and say, "this is a place to call your own." Like lions well perched on a well-positioned, self-assigned hilltop, little cats prefer high places, feeling safer at a height. Peace and warmth

Warm and daring, though unsafe and unconventional, this American Shorthair must pilot itself to a more acceptable napping place. Owner, Carol Rothfeld.

are also marked preferences; that is, a cosy spot, unblemished by human intervention and knowing. While it is infeasible to place the bed atop the kitchen stove or refrigerator, these oft-chosen napsites would assuredly be spoiled by a human's imposing or supposing that the cat sleep there.

Nevertheless, beds are excellent because they prevent wear and tear of furniture and help control stray hairs loosened by grooming, for the cat often grooms itself at its sleeping quarters. By observing the cat's preferred (reasonable) resting places and judiciously selecting a location for the bed, you may well strike a bargain with your feline. As necessity dictates, persistence and patience are the keys. Oftimes, leaving the bed in an off-the-wall spot may convince your cat to sleep in it—or at least by it.

Traveling crates, available at pet shops and pet supply houses, often can comfortably accommodate two felines, provided that the cats are on good terms with one another. These American Shorthairs are owned by Hedy Casperson.

CARNAGE ANYONE?

Without remorse for the unordinary or the mauled chipmunk in its clasp, a well-fed, owner-handled, best in show Siamese presents to its half-fainting owner its twitching catch. The necessity of capturing

While cats often enjoy the tickle and crunch of grasses and veggies, when it comes to eating, red meat is the unanimous choice.

Right: Domestic cats and wild cats alike are prime carnivores, that is, flesh eaters.
Below: Three seven-month-old Russian Blue kittens approach an open package of dry food. Owners, Ruth and Paula Nesenkar.

and hauling in neighborhood unrulies, mandated by feline serenity laws, overrides dormant instincts, full stomachs, and appalled owners' gagging. The cat's prey instinct, as immortal as the rat itself, manifests itself still in domestic felines, much to the dismay of mice and mice-fearing men.

The cat is a prime carnivore. All carnivorous animals require a diet that is based primarily on animal flesh, and the cat owner should consider this fact as requisite to the provision of a fine quality feline diet. Of course, flesh is high in protein and fats, but cats

do also require carbohydrates, vitamins, and minerals. Knowing what these various food terms actually mean and how they affect the cat contributes immensely to the responsible owner's understanding of his cat and its nutritional needs.

The wild cat hunts for its food. Although most cats have several preferred prey species, cats feed on the prey that is available, the prey that is near, the prey that is caught and consumed. Because of the variability of prey species, the cat must not have too rigid a nutritional need: while the flesh of one species may be high in certain amino acids and low in fat, that of another may be low in those same amino acids and relatively high in fat. The wild cat may have to feed on one or the other for a prolonged period of time, for any number of reasons. Of course, feeding on one specific prey species

Despite the hunting prowess and sheer power of the cougar, this giant cat is not a fussy eater. Over much of its range, mule deer comprises the mountain lion's diet.

Proper nutrition and well-balanced diets are paramount to proper kitten keeping. These teacup-sized Himalayans opt to be spoon-fed to healthy adulthood.

for a very long time is as unlikely as it is unhealthy; however, it does occur. Additionally, cats of many poverty-stricken regions around the world subsist on a diet largely of rice, cereals, and/or other such products. These cats, though in no way exhibiting the signs of health apparent in a properly fed feline, do survive. The cat, therefore, is and must be hardy, adaptable, and above all, not too fussy.

Young cats in the wild depend on instincts and mother to prescribe a balanced diet. A zoo-keeper has effectively intervened in providing a bottle for this tiger cub.

Yet owners are continually encouraged, by the variety of cat foods available and the cats themselves, not to fustigate a little feline fussiness. Many cats demonstrate peculiar, even bizzare, cravings: carrots, yogurt, cream cheese, kiwi, pretzels, etc. Giving in to our cat's seemingly preparturient wants should never replace a balanced diet, nor our own balance.

In recent years, some rights-of-animals awareness groups have proposed strictly vegetarian diets for the domestic cat. Though conceived with good intention, these diets have proven inadequate to the needs of the feline. The owner who opposes the consumption of flesh must consider that the cat's eating of flesh is as natural as the existence of the animal that it consumes. In other words, attempting to extract so vital a root as meat consumption from the cat is impossible and unhealthy.

A note regarding carbohydrates: cats in the wild do not eat plants, the primary source of carbohydrates, quite simply because they do not possess a digestive system that is capable of making use of carbohydrates. If felines require this foodstuff, then how do they acquire it? Cats feed primarily on herbivores, plant eaters. When the cat consumes its prey, it consumes the stomach and bowels and the contents therein, which in a herbivore assuredly is plant matter. Cats can and do make use of this partially digested carbohydrate matter. Some cats can be seen apparently eating grass, and some researchers believe that this is the cat's attempt to supplement its carbohydrate intake. Others, however, believe that grass serves as

Milk is a good source of protein and calcium, but should only be fed to the adult cat in moderation, since not all adult cats have enough of the enzymes necessary for the proper digestion of milk products. Birman owned by B.A. Cowles.

The good nutrition of any cat is manifested in the resilience and luster of its coat. Owner Linda Swierczynski surely feeds her Ragdoll well.

an emetic or hairball-extracting product. No study is conclusive, but most authorities believe that consuming grass should not evoke worry in the owner. Excessive or habitual grass consumption, however, should be addressed by a veterinarian.

Vitamins and minerals, many of which are not found abundantly in flesh, are acquired by the cat in much the same manner. Cats in the wild consume all or nearly all of the prey. They therefore ingest the internal organs, such as the liver and brain, which are high in many vitamins and minerals. Cats even consume the fur or feathers of the prey, which are not nutritionally enhancing but do serve as roughage. (The outstanding, discriminating exception is the bobcat, which "plucks" its prey.) In many cases, if the prey is small, the feline will consume the bones, thereby intaking a considerable amount of calcium and vitamin D.

The key to feline nutrition is balance. Providing a variety of meat products, with added carbohydrates, vitamins and minerals, is the

The sheen of the Chartreaux's coat results from proper eating, grooming and breeding. Owner, Geraldine V. Cox.

surest way to ensure proper feline nutrition. For the domestic cat owner in this modern world, feeding the feline is a task made easy. Manufacturers of feline food products have invested enormous sums of time and money to create the soundest nutritional product. Of course, there are exceptions, and one may find a poor product on any shelf. Veterinarians can provide knowledgeable advice regarding the cat food that best serves your individual cat. Most pet shops carry fine quality feeding products for the cat, and your local pet shop proprietor will be glad to assist you in your purchasing decision. However, responsible companies will either provide the nutritional information of the contents in their product or supply the inquiring owner with such information expediently upon request. Responsible owners will read the contents of the products that they feed to their charges.

Cats are sensible creatures with strong instincts. The Manx has thrived in human society for centuries close to man, who has facilitated its livelihood and sound health. Owner, Raymond R. Freiberger.

A green-eyed Maine Coon, owned by Karen Jacobus, displays the profuse coat which characterizes the breed. Eye luster and coat quality depend largely on proper feeding and care.

Above: From the largest Siberian tiger to the tiniest domestic cat, all felines need water. Fresh water is vital to the survival of all living animals. **Below:** Resting after a full supper, this lion cub resides contentedly.

FOOD FUNCTIONS

To understand why any given quantity or quality of food is recommended, it is important to understand the function that foods perform in the feline. In general, foodstuffs provide for three essential processes: tissue construction, cellular energization, and body insulation.

In assisting in tissue construction, food provides the essential building blocks from which all cells are made. Through the process of digestion, food is broken down into its most elemental components, and these vital little pieces are then reassembled in accordance with the structure of the tissue that they are to compose. For example, amino acids (nitrogeneous organic compounds) are the building blocks of proteins. When the cat ingests the flesh of an-

Kittens enthusiastically follow mother's lead. This shaded silver American Shorthair youth has been weaned successfully under its dam's watchful eye. Owner, Frosticat Cattery.

Solid-white Manx finds refuge in an A-frame. Owner, Barbara Haukenberry. Breeder, Mary E. Stewart.

other animal, the animal's proteins are broken down into their component amino acids. These then are reconstructed in an identical manner as the other proteinous tissues of the cat.

While the body is able to synthesize many of its necessary substances, many others must be obtained directly from foods. These necessary substances are vital to the successful functioning of the body's organs. Without them, progressive atrophy of the organs occurs, and soon life will cease. Incidentally, the energy required to conduct the digestive and syntheses processes is also the product of foodstuffs, which takes us to provision two.

Each cell, and in turn the entire body itself, needs energy for life to occur. Locomotion, thought, respiration, and indeed digestion itself are impossible without energy. As foods are broken down by the process known as oxidization, energy is released. This energy is used by the body for the efforts just described and unlistable others. Food energy that is not needed at any given moment can be stored by the body, and therefore food also provides energy for use at a later date, known as stored energy or energy reserve. This energy is stored as a fatty layer that is found just below the inner layer of skin, known as the   dermis. When needed, the fatty cells that compose the layer can be broken down, thereby causing the re-

Due to advances in modern pet science, there is no question as to how to feed your feline. Pet shops offer a wide variety of commercially prepared foods designed especially for your cat. Abyssinian youngster owned by Dean Mastrangelo.

lease of unusable energy. Additionally, the fatty layer serves as more than just a storage of energy reserves, which takes us to the third and final basic function of food.

The fatty layer, the result of unneeded energy, serves as a body insulator, providing both thermal and contact insulation. The fatty layer protects against the loss and gain of heat and cold, and thereby aids essentially in the regulation of the body's temperature. This thermally protective layer also helps the body to absorb the shocks accrued during normal existence, protecting the muscles, bones, and organs from bruises and other lesions.

Easily seen in this short and general explanation of the roles that food performs are the broad yet essential needs that foodstuffs fulfill. Taking it one step farther, one can easily understand why providing a sound feline diet is essential to the good health of the cat. Food is not simply food. Each foodstuff is independent of another, providing specific amounts of given nutrients; and each food group contributes differently to the good health of the cat.

An experimental breed known as the Wild Abyssinian, similar to the recognized Aby but allegedly closer in appearance to the original dwellers of Abyssinia, has "ticked" off many prominent Aby breeders and turned on others. Owners, Tord and Suzanne Svenson.

A full face perfectly balanced with the body gives the American Shorthair an unexaggerated, purebred appearance. Silver tabby owned by Carol Rothfeld.

Above: *The anatomy of the cat is designed more for jumping and speed than for endurance and continued stress. The average domestic cat can jump to heights many times its own height.* **Below:** *Discipline must begin when the cat is a kitten. Too many owners are so enamored by their cats' antics that, instead of correcting the animal, they run for their automatic cameras. Irene B. Brounstein is the owner of this photogenic Oriental Shorthair.*

CONDITIONAL CONDITIONING

Exercise is essential to achieve the optimum mental and physical states in the cat. Cats, lively and instinctive hunters, reap their exercise hours primarily through exploration. Cats do not require walks on a lead, and no cat has yet found much excitement on a monster-gerbil wheel. In fact, walks on a lead amble directly contrary to the feline nature. Restraint, coercion, never! Cats demand freedom, complete and unconditional. Though the lead-trained dog canters *adagio* figure eights and the horse and hamster each turns its given wheel, the cat needs more convincing inspiration to motivate its mechanisms. Exploration, intrigue, challenge, and a perceived end alert the feline sensibility.

Behaviorists agree that play is an important aspect in the development of many living creatures. The cat is no exception. The rules of the game apply to both football and life, for tigers and humans.

Despite your cat's innate curiosity and fascination with the outside world, responsible ownership dictates that domestic cats belong indoors, unless under the supervision of the keeper. Maine Coon cats exploring at the Schick Cattery of S.P. Bass.

A common owner crisis is the decision to let his cat roam. One may conclude that roaming, which embodies exploration, is essential to the achievement of the optimum feline. Such is certainly not the case, as the willing owner can provide the necessary stimulation for the cat within its home environment. A home with most of its area off-limits to the cat is not adequate, but the amenable home environment affords the cat suitable territory for exploration and conquest.

Cats exceptionlessly will not compromise their freedom and may not appreciate the new prospective of being locked inside: cats usually hate doors (except clear-glass or stained-glass ones). Some cats have been trained to walk on a lead, but these cats are exceptions, inconsistently and mostly momentarily cooperative. Unlike dogs, which perceive man's intentions as good and acceptable, cats will not succumb to the leather collar and chain. Yet, man has not given up this quest to lead-train the cat; it is usually children, however,

Above: Even if swimming does not make your feline's top-ten favorite activities, an open body of water poses real dangers to the domestic cat. Most cats have the natural ability to swim, though their endurance limits their ability to tread water for long periods. *Below:* Exploring the home of owner Raymond R. Freiberger are his two white Manx kittens.

Even the smallest kitten can upset the neighborhood gaggle.

that are seen pulling their stiffened and agitated, sidewalk-clasping kitten down the thoroughfare. Parents should instruct better. Hence, the authors do not recommend lead-training as a worthwhile venture or viable source of feline exercise.

Depending on square footage of "roaming" ground in the home, and, of course, the mice behind the walls, the degree to which the owner will have to amuse the cat will vary. Ideally, all owners spend time playing with their cat. Chasing a spool, pouncing on a leaf of paper, and other such diversions increase the feline-human bond and enhance the cat's human-owning experience. Although cats that lead solely indoor lives require considerably more of their owner's time to maintain peek physical condition than cats that are allowed to roam, indoor cats are struck by considerably fewer automobiles.

Though play is time-consuming to you, roaming is dangerous to your cat. Preventing the pigeon-coop-keeping ichthyologist from burlap-bagging your "blood-thirsty predator" and casting it into his garden pond is a legitimate concern in some communities. The outdoors pose infinite and unpredictable cat-harming and cat-hating possiblities. Parasites plague the woods. Cars crush. Dogs swallow whole. Rabbit-triggered traps snap indiscriminately on any unknowing furry passerby. Essentially, compared to the steel and cement which compose our twentieth-century world, cats are blamelessly too soft and squishable. And despite the cat's seeming contemplation of the world around it, it is not able to think, to decide, and to interpret. Instincts cannot rescue a lost cat from screeching rubber and steel nor determine the path furthest from harm's speedway.

The responsible cat owner must also consider the damages to the ecology of which cats are capable. The number of endangered bird species is considerable, and new species are continually added to

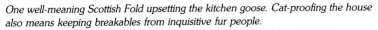

One well-meaning Scottish Fold upsetting the kitchen goose. Cat-proofing the house also means keeping breakables from inquisitive fur people.

the list. Cats can also prey on chickens, domestic rabbits and other small animals, and your neighbors who keep them would be less than pleased—thousands of cats have been shot by angry keepers. And thousands of others have been killed simply because they were cats.

The cat-loving humanitarian must consider that millions of cats are put to death as a result of the feline over-population. Letting your un-neutered queen or tom roam freely is irresponsible and very cruel.

The law-abiding citizen must realize that some areas actually prohibit cats from roaming, holding the owner responsible and casting the cat into feline prison with a possible death sentence (or nine?).

That roaming and hunting are part of the cat's nature is unquestionable. However, throughout much of this modern world, the territory is impossible for feline survival. The aforementioned "indestructible automaton" is assuredly destructible by more than just on-coming automobiles. The owner must weigh responsibly the decision to let the cat roam, based on these suggested considerations and his own strong feelings. As a last resort, lead-train the cat in front of your home.

Tree: Scratching post made by nature; one-way ladder to disorderly fledglings; well-rooted escape route from on-coming canines and other audacious ailurophobes.

Unless informed to the contrary, your cat (or cats) will claim any and all furniture as personal property. On owner Andre Jeannotte's favorite chair are two Havana Browns.

GROOMING CATS

Combs and brushes necessarily supplement the feline's daily grooming sessions. All cats, longhaired and short, are believed to preen themselves twenty times per day. Yet, owners must still pay regular attention to the coats of their cats. Domestic cats, without variance, are essentially small, pick-up-able animals that can be easily placed on a grooming table, or more agreeably (perhaps) on the owner's lap. Owners who opt for the latter shouldn't mind a little hair on their pants or skirts. Placing the cat on a table or other

The grooming instinct in all felines is strong: the cat family is industrious and thorough in its procedure. Cleaning and moistening the forepaw provides this lynx with a handy face-wipe.

waist-level platform, however, will keep your clothes somewhat hair-free and ease back strain too. On the table, lay whitish colored paper or cloth under the cat to check for parasites and other unwelcomes, as well as to catch fallen hairs. As most cats like attention, and kittens particularly, grooming sessions should commence when the cat is still a kitten in order to accustom it to the ritual. Regular sessions should be enjoyable for both brusher and brushee, and are healthful and habit-forming.

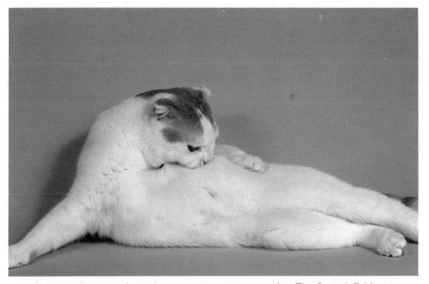

Cats typically groom themselves up to twenty times per day. This Scottish Fold twists itself to ensure that its entire coat has been cleaned. Owners, Gayle Rasmussen and June Young.

The Longhair With the cat situated comfortably, begin the grooming procedure by brushing the coat thoroughly in the direction of its lie, in order to loosen dirt, flaking skin, and other surface debris. With this accomplished, if the cat is not standing, bring the cat into a standing position and brush the undercat in the same manner as the uppercat was brushed. The lap-held cat may concede to laying on its back in order for its owner to brush its belly. The tail, the face, and the inner legs should all be brushed and combed gently and with care, as these are among the feline's most sensitive parts. (The use of a stiff-bristled toothbrush has been recommended in some cat literature.)

Now brush the entire cat again, this time against the lie of the fur. This particularly helps to remove dead coat. Again, brush the cat again in the direction of its lie. Brushing momentarily completed, a comb should now be employed in the same manner, brushing first

Unlike the Himalayan and Persian, the Birman possesses a long coat that does not mat. Cats without a dense undercoat need somewhat less grooming, although light daily brushings keep any cat's coat looking healthy. Owner, B.A. Cowles.

Young kittens instinctively understand the importance of good grooming habits.

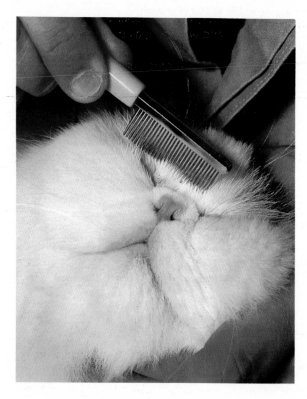

When combing the face of a cat, be sure to work gently and slowly. Persian, owned by Bob Fellman.

with the lie, against it, and with it again. If desirable, repeating with a fine comb the medium comb steps can contribute nicely to the final grooming achievement. With all combing done, a final brisk brushing should be given to the coat. The cat should now be allowed to give the final touches itself.

The Shorthair The coat composed of short hair requires considerably less time and brush strokes than that of long hair. Nonetheless, daily grooming contributes immeasurably to the overall health of the shorthaired coat. With the cat comfortable on the grooming table or stand, begin at the upper back and, working to the rear, give the entire upperbody a thorough brushing in the direction of the coat lie with a soft natural-bristle brush (preferable) or a comparable equivalent. Have the cat stand and brush the underbody in the same manner. The tail, the face, and the inner legs should all be brushed and combed gently and with care, as these are among the feline's most sensitive parts.

After the entire cat is brushed, the groomer may wish to repeat the process with a medium- or fine-toothed comb. Additionally, brushing and/or combing against the lie of the coat, always finishing, however, with a brushing with the lie, will aid in keeping the coat clean and neat. As an added touch to the coat, a chamois or silk cloth can be used to bring out a special shine. As with the longhaired cat, the shorthair should be allowed (for who's to stop it) to give its coat the final, personal touches.

A slicker brush can be used to help break up mats on double-coated cats such as the Maine Coon. Owner, Jean Hannum.

Bathing

A vast majority of domestic felines live out their days without ever entering the world of the bath—and surely their owners are grateful, for the cat being bathed can prove hell in the making. The bath, however, does have its role in the feline world. Show cats in particular require bathing, as do those house pets who find their way to the rear end of an angry skunk or the bottom of a smelly garbage can. In most cases, a dry bath is all that is necessary, and such are generally more accepted by even the most hesitant cats. If brushing has become a regular ritual, the dry bathing should prove little more effort entailing. Dry baths (available at pet shops) typically require little more than a sprinkling on and a brushing out. Besides for cleaning purposes, dry baths can also be used to curtail parasite infestation.

Wet baths, conversely, are typically major cat aversions, even to the best and most regularly groomed specimens. If a wet bath is

A medium- and fine-toothed metal comb is a useful grooming tool on both long- and short-coated cats. Accustomed to the grooming procedure is a well-balanced Balinese.

The Ragdoll typically requires less grooming than other longhaired cats, although daily sessions are recommended. Owner, Dean Mastrangelo.

necessary, the owner is advised to wear protective gloves that will guard against scratching. A basin often proves more acceptable to the cat than does either the sink or bathtub. Once the bathing process is underway, with any luck, the cat will concede to its lathering owner's wishes. Wet cats know when they are beat and usually co-

Black smoke and white Cornish Rex owned by Mary Theresa and Joel Singer. The Rex does not need to be brushed as do most other cats. A once-over with a flannel cloth proves sufficient for keeping the coat in optimum condition.

Requiring more grooming attention than other felines, the luxuriantly coated Persian requires extensive daily brushings, as well as an occasional bath.

operate. The near-comical helplessness of a wet feline, an animal who prides itself on its stunning appearance and demeanor, begs the cat's side expertly. Wasting time is not recommended, since trying a cat's patience in this most vulnerable state can leave both of you unhappy and wet. In the case of certain untolerating, persistent, dirty felines, it may be best to leave the bathing to a professional groomer or veterinarian.

If wet bathing is to become a regular part of the cat's life, it should then be initiated at a young age and performed with some regularity, guarding, of course, against drying of the coat and skin.

More common perhaps than bathing is the application of coat and skin conditioners. Essentially the cat is a self-cared-for animal. But, especially in the longhaired breeds, many cats do well to have a conditioner applied to them during grooming. These preparations are available at pet shops, or for special needs can be prescribed by a veterinarian.

SPECIAL PARTS

In addition to the coat and skin, special grooming attention must be paid to the cat's eyes, ears, nose, and teeth. In conjunction with the grooming procedure, either before or after, the owner should check these parts. The eyes should be checked for excessive tearing, clarity, mucus, and a build-up of debris in the corners of the eyes. Excessive tearing or mucus build-up can signal infection, and a veterinary check-up may be in order. Unclear eyes are a part of old age, which is often accompanied by cataracts and other eye conditions;

Left: Reveling rebelliously in its saber-tooth ancestors, this domestic snarls convincingly.

Opposite: The combination of the cat's tremendous balance, strong retractible claws and physical agility makes it an admirable tree-climber. Domestics and wilds alike can be arboreal in nature, though wilds typically have an easier time climbing down.

again, a veterinary check-up may be in order. Debris in the eye should be removed with a soft cotton swab, preferably moistened with sterile water or mineral oil. The cleaned eye should be checked regularly for the next few days to make certain that debris does not recur, which can lead to discomfort, irritation, and possible infection.

The ears should be checked for cleanliness. A build-up of wax is common, and wax should be removed from the outer ear with a

*Despite the Devon Rex's less-than-usual appearance, the breed does not pose un-
usual health problems to its owner. Owner, Lisa Bressler.*

cotton swab, moistened with isopropyl alcohol or an ear-cleaning
solution. Though mites do not plague the cat as they do the dog,
the presence of brown wax in the ear should be viewed immedi-
ately by a veterinarian. Do not rely on home or over-the-counter
remedies, as unless the condition is diagnosed, these can prove
more harmful than helpful. Care must be exercised so as not to
probe into the ear, which can lead to injury or complication. Additionally, no one swab should enter both ears, as such practice,
though frugal, can easily spread infection from one ear to the other.
Chronically dirty ears deserve veterinary inspection.

The nose should be checked for discharged moisture and
warmth. A runny nose can be a sign of a bacterial or viral infection.
A dry or excessively moist nose, as well as a cold or hot nose, can

also be a sign that something is askew in the harmony of the cat's functioning.

The cat's teeth should all be free from tartar and plaque and be fully intact. Missing or chipped teeth may require special treatment by a veterinarian. But, at the very least, the owner should investigate the cause of their poor condition. Chipped teeth often signal a poor diet, often lacking in calcium. Tartar and plaque accumulation should be removed periodically by a trained professional, as such accumulations can lead to gum disease and tooth decay. Owners of longhaired cats should be particularly aware of the possible entangling of fur around the cat's teeth. Such accumulation results in foul-smelling breath and the loss of teeth, if left unattended.

Except for breeding, the Manx is a totally normal cat—this tailed antediluvian house dweller has remained indoors since Noah's hasty doorslam. This Manx is surely the max, owned by Shelly Page.

Some owners opt to clip their cat's front claws to limit damage to furniture. Extra long claws can cause splayed feet or damaged paw pads if left unattended. Most usually, cats groom and file their toenails by themselves. Owners should not clip too closely so as to avoid cutting the quick, the nail's blood vessel. Egyptian Mau, owned by Andre Jeannotte.

The Ocicat is an athletic though graceful animal prized for its well-spotted agouti coat and marked vitality. Silver Ocicat owned by Rebecca Nan.

CLAWS

The cat's claws typically require little care from the owner. Cats usually keep their foreclaws in good condition by scratching and clawing objects, which can range from the trunks of trees to pop's easy chair; cats maintain their hind claws by biting the old outer casings of the nails. Scratching is often erroneously interchanged with sharpening; in fact, sharpening the claws is but a small part of the reason cats scratch.

The claws are composed of hundreds of layers of cells, like a human's (or cat's) skin; cells die continuously and are replaced by new ones. Dead claw cells dull the claws and the cat scratches to remove this well-worn outer casing. It is not quite the same as sharpening your own nails or a kitchen knife, more so it is like a reptile that brushes against rocks or trees to shed its outer scales.

Full-sized ears and eyes, complemented by prominent cheekbones, give the Devon Rex a "pixielike" appearance. Owner of this expressive blue tabby kitten is William A. Leisentritt.

In addition to "sharpening" or honing the nails, scratching serves other purposes in the cat community. The cat's clawing objects also serves as a means to mark its territory, especially with the males; this behavior is akin to the male deer's (buck's) marking of tree trunks with its antlers. Stomping and strumming the paws in time triggers cat's scent glands and leaves its "monogram" on furniture, sweaters, linen, curtains, etc. Scratching, too, is plain and simple good grooming and a large part of the cat's psychological wholeness and routine. While the cat's scratching instinct cannot and should not be eliminated, it can, however, be curtailed and honed.

Providing a scratching post is the first step to directing the cat's clawing instinct. Discipline contributes as well to the cat's understanding of your intentions. It has been purported that cats opt to claw your favorite chair because it is yours and thus marked by your scent. Placing an old garment of yours (possibly unlaundered?) on the post may impel the cat to use the post.

An articulate and composed Abyssinian sits in its owner's favorite chair, a tasteful, scentful setting for this portrait. Owner, Linda B. Jones.

Above: *This white-footed hybrid is the Snowshoe, developed recently from Siamese–American Shorthair crosses. Body type favors the American Shorthair in some specimens, or appears more foreign in others. The "snowshoes" are believed to be created by a spotting gene. Owner, Doris Chin Reese.* **Below:** *The Oriental Shorthair is essentially a self-colored Siamese. These cats distinguish themselves for their undeniable beauty and warm personality.*

Particularly if your cat dwells indoor–outdoor, declawing cannot be considered. As mechanisms of defense, escape, and movement, the cat's claws are vital. Chartreaux.

Some owners, unable or unwilling to guide the cat's instincts, consider having their cats declawed, which is the surgical procedure by which the claws are removed. Heated arguments are unsheathed both for and against the declawing of cats. Before an owner casts the final decision to declaw a cat, he should be reminded of the psychological damage incurred by this loss; not to mention (but to mention), it is painful for the cat and requires that the cat be off his "unfamiliar" and hurting paws for a good week. The cat's need to feel the security of being able to defend itself and provide for itself is furnished by its claws. Even if your indoor Himalayan isn't on mouse-patrol or out combatting the neighborhood pit bulls, its claws still contribute to its complete felinity: the cat rests

Korat, the revered cat of Thailand, rests peacefully, bringing good luck to its owner's home.

contentedly knowing that it could work over the lowly rodent or cocky pit bull should the need arise. That these survivor instincts are still extant in the domestic cat speaks well of the need to keep our cats' claws. Domestication surely has not exorcised much of the "wild" from our apartment and condo companions.

If, however, the cat and the owner are incompatible solely because of the former's claws, taking into consideration the millions of homeless cats, then declawing may be a responsible option, for likely the cat is better in a home without its claws than on the street

Cats and dogs, when acquainted, can live together in harmony—however, should dissonance arise, the cat's claws act as a well-honed deterrent. A well-mannered Samoyed puppy and American Shorthair kittens.

The appeal of the American Curl is singular. This young bicolor captivates the heart and imagination of owner Geri Hamilton on a daily basis.

with them. Truly, declawing is a decision that rests with the owner, and the authors hope that it will be made responsibly and not hastily.

VETERINARY VISITATION

All cat keepers must choose a veterinarian who will provide specialized care for their pets and sound advice to them as proprietors. Choosing the veterinarian should not be based solely on price or convenience, though these are important considerations. In selecting your pet specialist, you must consider his specialty and preferred animals and your comfort with him. Though veterinarians study a wide range of animals types, most choose to concentrate, for one reason or another, on a specific animal or two. Ideally, the veterinarian you choose has a strong background in cats and a sincere love of animals. Additionally, the pet owner should be comfortable with the veterinarian so that questions are not hesitant and advice is not misunderstood. If your prospective vet consistently talks over your head and is unable to communicate with you clearly, find another vet (or get a smart relation to go to the office with you). Choosing a veterinarian is an important pet owner's decision, for

Healthy blue-point mitted Ragdoll, owned by Georgann Chambers. A keen knowledgeable eye, supplemented with regular veterinary visits, provides the best policy for feline health.

When first visiting the vet with your new charge, whether a kitten or a cat, be sure to bring along a copy of the health records provided by the seller or previous owner.

ideally the pet will receive care throughout its lifetime from the same vet, who will come to know the cat well as the years progress.

Inoculations and tests are provided and conducted on a regular schedule, beginning at the kitten's young age, often six weeks. Your veterinarian can best advise you on when these inoculations and tests should be conducted and which specific test or vaccine should be used. Therefore, it is important to have your veterinarian chosen before you select your pet-to-be, whether kitten or adult.

The alert, responsive eyes of this brilliant black Bombay, owned by Janet Becker, suggest proper care and upkeep, which entail sound nutrition, adequate exercise, and plenty of tender loving.

Ebony and ivory, simple harmony, a black and a white Cornish Rex. Potentially fall-ing on unexpecting ears, a hanging plant looms above. Nearly all common house-plants prove toxic to cats if eaten and must be kept well away from the feline.

"No, no, not the dip!" Owners must be particularly careful about flea preparations when caring for young kittens. Talk to a vet and read the package instructions.

PLAGUES AND PARASITES

The healthy cat without question displays its health in its vigor, clear and alert eyes, healthy coat, and good appetite. The ailing cat, however, shows various signs depending on the condition and its degree of severity. Diseases, ailments, and parasites can serve as three major groupings of the ill conditions that affect the feline.

The first group, the disease, is by far the most dreaded by the cat owner. The mere mention of feline leukemia, enteritis, or rabies runs chills up the owner's spine. Fortunately for today's owner, diagnosis, treatment, and prevention of many feline diseases is well researched and readily available. Most importantly, the owner must provide his cat with prompt veterinary care. Before the new cat is purchased, it is recommended that you contact a veterinarian for a schedule of vaccinations and immunizations; also helpful is an approximated cost. Then, after you bring your new charge home, follow the veterinarian's advice.

Of course, there are many diseases for which vaccines do not exist. The keys then become prevention and prompt treatment. Prevention first entails a sound diet. Cats are naturally hardy animals with strong immune systems. Feeding the cat nutritiously goes a long way in preventing illness. The second key to prevention is observation. The cat should receive a good looking over every day. This "check-up" can be done before or after grooming, and the

The Colorpoint Shorthair, like most other Oriental breeds, exhibits a svelte, lithe body type. Accurately assessing your cat's condition requires a clear perception of the ideal breed specimen. Seal-tortie-point Colorpoint Shorthair, owned by Irene B. Brounstein.

two can therefore be knocked out in one quick sitting. Things to be checked include lumps and growths, either above or below the skin (common signs of cancer); swelling to any body part (common sign of infection, edema, digestive or kidney disorder); opaque, distant, or unresponsive eyes (the most universal sign that something is wrong); poor coat (poor diet or parasites); and general lethargy (another common and universal sign). If any signs occur that signal to you, the observant and responsible owner, that something is astray or amiss in your feline, don't hesitate to contact your veterinarian. He will offer you the most sound advice on the specific condition as best as he can ascertain by your report. He may well recommend that you bring your cat in for a more thorough check and/or testing. Again, don't hesitate, as early diagnosis and treatment are the essentials of recovery. In addition, don't hesitate to get a second opin-

A solid build, healthy coat, and alert responsiveness are all positive signs of good health. American Shorthair, silver mackerel tabby, owned by Terry Havel.

Without motivation, the cat may revert to a solely sedentary existence. Springing your cat into action, with a ball, a string, a toy, helps to keep the cat healthy, happy, and strong. Somali, owned by S. Goldberg.

ion from another veterinarian if for any reason you doubt the first—the owner's instincts are often to be trusted.

The second group, the ailment, includes such conditions as vomiting, diarrhea, heart trouble and breathing difficulty, and numerous others. Very often these conditions are the symptoms and signs and not the actual condition. For example, the owner taking her cat with chronic diarrhea to the vet may learn that the cat is suffering from a viral or bacterial infection of the lower intestinal tract, or on the other hand it may be a dietary insufficiency, or it may be an allergic reaction. Breathing difficulty can signal cancer, inhalation pneumonia, emphysema, bronchitis, or another condition. In short, though the cat is essentially a healthy (or sickless) animal, ailments are numerous, and ailments often are the signs and not the condition. As with diseases, observation that leads to early diagnosis and prompt treatment is the key to maintaining the cat's good health.

Above: *The folded ears of a Scottish Fold can hide the early signs of ear infection. Regular ear inspection must therefore find its way into the daily grooming procedure. Scottish Fold, owned by Michael E. Nelson.* **Facing page:** *Well-maintained Turkish Van displaying its clean ears, clear eyes and health-conveying nose.*

The third group, the parasites, is by far the most familiar and detested. Parasites lurk in grasses, hide in carpets, and jump from coat to coat. Fleas and ticks are the most commonly known parasites, and they are easily detected by the owner. Take time during the daily grooming session to check for fleas and ticks. They typically are found on the skin itself. Fleas, tiny jumpers, are much more mobile than the pot-bellied, slow-motion ticks. However, both are often found in the body's crevices, e.g., behind the ears, in a fold of the neck or in the pits of the limbs. Be sure to check the entire cat thoroughly. Fleas are best eliminated with a flea-killing preparation, either powder or spray. Be sure to use only flea and tick killers that are made especially for cats, as others may cause serious, even lethal, complications. When embedded, ticks can be removed with tweezers turned in a twisting motion, so as to prevent the embedded head from remaining behind and causing infection. The appli-

cation of a smothering substance, such as petroleum jelly, has also proven helpful in forcing the tick to retract from the cat's skin, after which it can be removed with ease.

Mange, caused by parasitic mite infestation, appears as balding patches. The skin will appear red and raw, and the cat will scratch often, often incessantly. As with other parasite infestations, prompt treatment is necessary. Ringworm, a fungus, is often confused with mange or other parasitic infestations. Signs of ringworm include balding and/or lesions, and the infection requires prompt veterinary treatment.

Besides external parasites, many internal parasites feed on the cat. Internal parasites include whipworms, roundworms, tapeworms, and intestinal protozoa, to name but a few. Many parasitic infestations, including most of the more common ones, can be easily diagnosed and treated by today's veterinarian. Some signs include weight loss, weakness, abdominal swelling, lethargy, difficulty in passing stool or diarrhea, and labored breathing. As can be seen, however, these signs are considerably varied, and some are even contradictory, thus the importance of veterinary diagnosis. Through testing and observation, the condition can be detected and most likely treated successfully.

Owners of longhaired cats may find that their grooming ability does not suffice to protect against parasites and other feline undesirables. Professional grooming services can be of great assistance in these cases. Persian, owned by Carol Duncan.

The standard of perfection for the Scottish Fold breed calls for a cat of exceptional strength and durability—characteristics in keeping with the rugged Scotch ancestors of the breed.

Raw spit and the survival of the species: a raspy Bengal roars a proclamation of its unashamed felinity: "vivat"—life to the everlasting cat! Owner, Tina Woodworth.

Drama, Scratches & Litters

Top: Domestic to a point: Bengal unfurling its claws. *Bottom:* Lioness and cub from her litter.

Cement walls, daytime dividers of suburbanites, their untied dogs and children, are clawed upon and climbed upon by untidy, tangy strays. Aroused by the aromatic sublimity of late spring, indivisible feral felinity, the male of the species, clamor and curr, crying and groaning, growling and droning, purr, purr, bray, troat, screech, screech, scream. The neighbors interrupt, the window slams. Crick, chirr, churr, coo, coo. Shout. Chat unlike cats, spring-inspired ado: such fuss. Caw, cluck, clang, croak?—uncatlike, uncanny utterances from the disturbed "pack" Honk, squall, growl, growl, growl. Shout! Yip, yap, yup—elated ululation from the undulating fur mass.

The near-pornographic display of city cats responding unneuteredly, with enviable virility, to the female's immodest needs is cacophonous, though gracefully harmonious with the nature of both wild and domestic cats. Deciphering the unorchestrated glob, male mauling male, mewing and moaning, defies our orderly, semi-civilized human society. In cat terms, however, brawling for the queen's paw and acceptance is akin to survival. Nature has well devised this feline battle royal, and the betterment and progeneration of the species depends upon it.

The drama of the mating institution is never more pronounced than in wild cats; this highly ritualized episode, in its thought-evoking detail, conjures unmistakable images of the behavior of our domestic cats, instincts sustained through centuries of domestication.

In the domestic breeding program, the owner orchestrates, to an extent dictates, the resultant offspring. Color breeding, especially with Persians, always has its surprises.

A majestic tiger intakes vast territory with its sense of sight and smell: at first hint of an intruder's infringement on claimed hunting and mating grounds, the tiger resounds a persuasive admonition.

In the wild or an unattended suburb, the mature female, without crimson or regret, will naturally attract a number of males to joust for her hand and union. The female typically will not accept any male's offering until his worthiness is proven. The first male to arrive may setup camp within the female's territory, patiently awaiting his challenger while displaying his self-convinced strength and power. When a challenger arrives, chests are expanded, ruffs are furled, and the joust commences. Combat is fierce and diaphramatic in its brilliance and conviction. Fatalities are not common, but serious injury is an assumed risk. The joust typically ends with one male retreating, scratched, dusty, and more personally than physically scarred. The defeated does not surrender his general bid, however, and will either retire to a nearby vantage point, awaiting a potential opportunity, or venture on in search of a land where the other cats are less impressive or the luck is more to his favor. The rolling of dice, however, does not really determine the outcome of battle. The sparring that felines undertake is a vital part of a selection process designed to propagate the species by generating only the finest quality offspring. It is not always the supreme victor that mates with the queen; she may so appreciate one cat's display that she will encourage him to mate with her. Such a decision, however, entails the indefinite risk of angry rebuttal from a victor. The usual scenario involves a dominant male who, exhausted by continued victorious bouts, eventually succumbs to the fiery fresh newcomer and is nonetheless awarded the queen's favors.

The victor of the first battle remains to face the second challenger. On the battles rage, each time with the victor remaining and the queen indifferently observing. When she feels that it is time, she may gracefully come to her paws and begin to leave the battle site slowly. If the tom does not follow, she will slow and then stop. The tom almost inevitably follows within a short time unless he is hurt badly. As the queen walks she rubs her head and body against surrounding objects. As the tom follows, he too rubs his body against the same objects as did the queen, while he speaks to her cooingly.

Competition is not over; it takes new form. The weary yet determined male must now address, tête á tête, the hesitating queen. If he approaches too quickly, too suddenly, she defends against encroachment, with hisses, snarls, claws displayed. The tom responds humbly with unbending respect, unexpectingly. He vocalizes his desires patiently and repeatedly. Assured of his intentions, she permits his approach; noses and paws establish the acquaintance. She suggests readiness but commonly will cast several more refusals, each further humbling the oncoming tom. She will eventually acquiesce. She will roll over, starting and finishing on her belly, remain there, and press her hindquarters into the air. He will mount, seizing her neck with his teeth, grasping her shoulders with his forelegs and her hindquarters with his own, and perchance treading upon her with his hind paws while she treads the ground with hers. Coitus occurs in very short sessions, each ending with an astonishing cry from the female, after which she paw-swipes the male, retreats a short distance, and grooms herself consistently.

Blue male Abyssinian with his get: ruddy Aby kittens. Color inheritance, the way in which colors are passed from parents to offspring, remains a considerable frontier in the world of science.

Coitus occurs repetitively. Soon again the queen accepts the male. All is repeated. Again she encourages him to mount. Coitus in this manner can continue for two to four days, even with domestics. Coitus can occur as frequently as ten times per hour for the first few hours. Not uncommonly the first male becomes exhausted and retires, and a second male is accepted by the female. The female is often more receptive now, in her high state of excitement, and the second male may escape many of the struggles undertaken by the first. (Queens can carry a litter sired by more than one male, with no detriment to either them or their offspring.) Soon now the female's receptivity diminishes and she refuses any further approaches. She begins home. Her estrus continues for several hours, but she adamantly refuses any more champions. She returns home.

Thus, courtship in the wild reveals much about the nature of the cat and the nature with which domestic cats must necessarily approach even the most laboratorylike breeding program. The described courtship ritual applies in general to most all felids. The best-dressed Persians, Siamese, or Shorthairs, if left to their own accord, would inevitably court, mate, and reproduce in a fashion not so unlike the described. Additionally, the bothersome arrangements, travel and contacts, tom fees and contracts, would all be completely eliminated. Unfortunately, in a few generations, all of our domestic cats would revert to a feral state, essentially looking the same and refusing to participate in exhibition.

The continuation and improvement of domestic breeds, however, could not possibly rely on our cats to pick and choose, to fight and

Depending on the registry, the Burmese can be sable (brown) only or brown, champagne, platinum, or blue. Breeds are created and maintained by man: the meaningful, though seemingly arbitrary, delineation of the Burmese colors well exemplifies this fact.

Selective breeding demands the consideration of all genetic characteristics and their interplay upon each other. Two copper-eyed white Persians (Longhairs), owned by Corpolonga Cattery.

roam, without a little help from humans. Breeds, by definition, are sustained and maintained by men, not cats (though cats do help). No serious breeding program could be left to the finicky queen rejecting a line-up of toms from all over the district, state, or country. Yet the queen does express her hesitation in our organized orgy. Likewise allowing champion-producing breeder-toms to fight for the right to a proven queen would hardly be acceptable to the owners of any animal involved.

Disregarding the authors' scandalous scenario, the selection of the appropriate mate must be based upon the breeder/owner's careful study of the available stock. Of course, not every mature, receptive queen is mated, as may occur in the wild. Because the natural selection process is eliminated, the advancement and survival of the domestic breed rests on the responsibility and competence of the breeder. Breeding breeds is not to be taken lightly.

THE QUEEN IN HER HEAT

Cats are induced ovulators, which means that queens release eggs to be fertilized only when encouraged to do so, whether it be by mechanical or other means. The mechanical is, of course, the physical: the stimulation of the male's penis elicits the reaction of the queen's egg release. The other stimulus of ovulation is considered psychological, for the follicles can ripen, though the eggs are not released until coitus, without physical stimulation. Dogs, conversely, are spontaneous ovulators. This important difference means that whereas the bitch in heat exhibits outward physical signs, the queen demonstrates her heat only with her changed behavior. Addition-

The Persian breed, one of the most highly and selectively bred of all domestic breeds, still adheres to behavioral effects elicited by the estrus cycle, as experienced by all female cats.

The Maine Coon breed was subject to many years of natural selection in the wilds of the northeastern United States. Maine Coon, silver classic tabby and white, owned by Connie Webb.

ally, dogs typically have twice-occurring estrus periods, and the bitch's coming into heat therefore can be calculated to some degree of accuracy; cats, however, are polyestrus and can experience up to four estrus cycles annually (though two to three cycles is average) during their prime physical years. Essentially what all this means is that manipulating and controlling the mating are both more and less possible in cats than in other domestic pets: the queen can be induced to mate and ovulate when given the appropriate physical and mental stimulation at most times during her mature years; she can also, however, mate and conceive with most any male during one of her cycles if confronted with him, regardless of her owner's desire or intention.

The queen will normally experience her first estrus cycle between the age of five and nine months, but this varies considerably from breed to breed and individual to individual. Reported is a female's coming into heat at age three months and another's not finding her first heat upon her until age 13 months. In part the first heat is controlled by the birth date of the cat. Heat cycles commonly hit the domestic female three times a year, once in the spring, once in the summer, and once in the fall. Therefore, a kitten born in the late autumn is more likely to ovulate early than another that was born in mid-summer, both ovulating sometime in the spring.

This well-coated cat will experience the same degree of climatic variables that affect the estrus cycles of all felines. Smoke tortie Persian, owned by Cindy Swartz.

The concept of three annual cycles, like that of the age of maturation, does have its variables. Cats of the colder climes may have only one cycle per year; cats of the temperate zones, two to three; and cats inhabiting warm regions, three to four. It is safe to say that a majority of domestic felines experience three estrus cycles, which differs from one, the typical number of estrus cycles witnessed in wild felids. This difference is believed to have a direct relationship to the domestication process. Additionally, the domestic queen's estrus cycle can be controlled by supplying artificial daylight for time periods similar to those of her natural season (12 to 14 hours). In this way "winter" litters can be created. In general, no queen should be mated before she is at least one year of age.

Heat typically lasts between three and six days, recurring at approximately 14-day intervals until the queen experiences a conceptionary mating or the "winter" season ends. Throughout the several-day heat, hormonal levels gradually grow, and with their growth comes a sharpening change in behavior. Signs of heat include audible beckoning calls, which clearly tell male cats that she is ready to mate; general restlessness, and an increased desire to be outdoors. Other common though not foolproof signs are increased affection towards the owner and a coupling of tail twitching, raising the hindquarters and treading the ground with the hind feet. It is not uncommon for the queen to spend increasing amounts of time in a fore-down, hind-up position, often while pushing her chin against the floor and purring, only to stop suddenly, role from belly to belly, and begin washing herself. If not guarded carefully, the queen will likely disappear for several days and not return until mated to some tom.

Eight-month-old black female Persian. The coming of the first heat depends to some extent on the season in which the cat was born as well as the climate of the cat's geographic locale.

The Exotic Shorthair resulted when American Shorthair breeders crossed to "prepotent" Persians to improve the overall type of the Shorthair. Tortoiseshell kitten owned by Benjamin Thomas.

The Exotic Shorthair occurs in a myriad of color possibilities; most colors accepted for the Persian and the American Shorthair are also acceptable for the Exotic.

The female enters heat and evidences signs of her condition up to several days prior to actual mount-assuming readiness. This fact traces to the wilds, in which males are necessarily given several days notice to make their way to her territory (often far from their own) and stake their rough-and-tumble trickery and tact for the glory of the queen. Seasoned owners speak words of wisdom to new cat-fancy participants: living through the queen in heat is an experience one never forgets.

Especially with "regulars" (cats of no defined breed), queens may go through a behavioral metamorphosis, clinging to screens, hanging from curtains—quickly tattering—and the flailing pant legs of aghast family members. Don't hasten to the door, and don't be harsh, as correction is rarely effective. Rather understand the hormonal changes that are occurring within the queen, that these are natural and stem from the intense desire shared by all species to propagate their kind.

If mating is desired, by all means this is the time to bring the queen to her mate—or her mate to her. If mating now and in the future is not the desire then neutering should be seriously considered. If mating is desired, but not for some time, the owner can do little but grin—if rather chagrined it be.

THE CRYING QUEEN The cry, screech, or yell emitted by the feline female, domestic and wild, after mating has intrigued man for many an age. In simplicity, it is believed to be caused by the "spines" of the penis, which are tiny bonelike structures that protrude invertedly (in such a way that they run counter to the force of the penis when withdrawn) along the penis. These spines are be-

*Above: Despite the rex and many other mutations which have contributed to the variety of today's cat breeds, all cats still adhere to the basic principles of felinity, such as induced ovulation. Cornish Rex, bred by Alexis Chontos and owned by Ms. Chontos with Shannon Koyama. **Opposite:** The Himalayan resulted in the early part of the twentieth century from various Siamese, Birman, and Persian crosses. This blue-pointed Himalayan is owned by Geri Hamilton.*

lieved by many to be an evolutionary adaptation that better enables felines to conceive in their induced-ovulation propagation existence. The spines are not common in mammals and are found only in induced ovulators (though not all induced ovulators have them), which lends itself well to supporting the evolutionary theory just described. Whether or not they are the cause or trigger of egg release, their being the cause of the cry is very believable.

Those of us tired of sterile science cooling our conceptions can rely on the statement made in the seventeenth century by Edward Topsell: that the female lets out a cry is " . . . because his seed is so fiery hot, that it almost burneth the female's place of conception."

Induced ovulation is an evolutionary advantage to solitary creatures. (Excepting the lion, felids are essentially solitary animals.) Many terrains found throughout the felid distribution range are quite hostile to feline existence, whether because of food shortages or extensive predation, or other circumstances. Therefore, cats in the wild, living their solitary lives, are often spread out over considerable distances, commonly several acres or more. The life of the average feline egg after it is released is approximately 24 hours. Leaving to chance in the wild that copulation would occur on that very day is extremely risky for the survival of the species. Sperm on the other hand has an after-release life of approximately 72 hours. Therefore, eggs not released in the female until after coitus has occurred bear the advantage of increased likelihood of fertilization. Coitus stimulates the release of the one-day eggs, which are typically three to five in number.

Despite numerous matings, it is possible that the domestic female does not conceive. In such instances, estrus will either continue, with the queen again becoming receptive to toms, or it will discontinue but soon return, spurring the queen to receptivity. Failed conception can be caused by physical and/or mental conditions. The queen, though receiving adequate physical stimulation, may not have received the requisite mental stimulation to ripen the follicles, which in turn release the eggs. It is believed that, in domestic felines especially, familiarity breeds affection (or at least litters), since second matings prove successful believably because the queen is more mentally stimulated because of her familiarity (trust?) with the tom. If a second mating proves barren, there may be some complication in the reproductive system that is preventing the production of eggs, their release, their travelling the fallopian tubes, etc.

Ann Baker, originator of the Ragdoll breed, believes that the Ragdoll does not breed like other domestic cats, which is her reason for trademarking the breed. Ragdoll owned by Linda Swierczynski.

Turkish Vans are not considered prolific breeders, having an average litter size of four. Evenso, male Vans, true to feline masculinity, will mate the year 'round.

THE TOM IN HIS GLORY

In the seventeenth century, the famed feline observer Edward Topsell spoke, "In the time of their lust they are wilde and fierce, especially the males, who . . . will not keepe the house: at which time they have a peculiar direfull voyce."

Mr. Topsell sketches well the behavior of the mature tom who senses a calling queen. Toms will intensively attempt to free themselves of the home, and if successful they will almost inevitably engage in battle over the queen.

Toms are ready to mount the year 'round, which is not an uncommon fact with males of the mammal group. It is the female that dictates when and where copulation occurs, which is also a common mammalian characteristic. An essential difference between cats

Knowledge and planning are required in all breeding programs, especially in breeds with mutations associated with undesirable conditions.

and many other mammals is that toms do not court the female until she first demonstrates sexual willingness. At all other times the tom lives his life in feline delicacy. While toms will engage in territorial disputes with other cats, these battles are highly ritualistic and cannot cast even a shadow on the intensity of the combat undertaken for mating rights.

Like the "coming of age" in the queen, the age of sexual maturity for the tom varies from breed to breed and from individual to individual. Puberty commences in the domestic female typically between her fourth and fifth month of life, and she is physically able to mother a litter typically by her ninth month of life (although 12 to 24 months is a much safer age for the queen). The tom begins puberty at roughly the same age (four to five months), but his achieving maturity is a considerably slower process. Whereas domestic toms may be capable of siring a litter as early as their sixth month of age, and whereas toms under the age of six months may display an interest in sex play, domestic toms typically are not sexually prepared for fatherhood until their 12th to 18th month, with the average being the 15th month. As a note to potential breeders, both queens and toms commonly prove their novice in first performances; but, by the second season, they display the sharpness of their instincts.

The watershed of puberty commonly concurs with the diminished rate of growth in the cat. Though they will continue to accumulate bulk, both toms and queens have generally reached their height and length potentials when their glands start the increased trickle of sex hormones.

Early sex play should not be considered as necessarily abnormal, even if this behavior takes the form of mounting people or inani-

The Manx's taillessness, like the Scottish Fold's folded ear and the Cornish Rex's guardhairless coat, was the result of a spontaneous mutation, a change which occurred naturally, without human intervention.

Pair of cheetahs surveying a grassy terrain. Cheetahs tend to form loose social groups, often hunting in pairs, which differs from both the pride-forming nature of the lion and the essentially solitary existence of most other cats.

mate objects. In most all cases this behavior should be considered as nature preparing the tom for his future role as sire. It is only when the behavior continues well into maturity and occurs with frequency that the tom should be regarded as questionable as a stud. The mature tom, when he senses that a female in heat is nearby, spray-marks his territory and tries untiringly to escape the confines of the house to meet with the beckoning queen. Spraying his territory and determined attempts to mate with the female are normal; they are not signs of sexual depravity.

Toms typically have two forms of territory: one which they wish to have exclusive control over and which they will defend at high cost; and a second which is held as uncontested roaming ground, to be shared by many cats of the area. The entire combined territory can span five acres, but a considerably smaller territory is more common. The female typically has a small territory, and she often prefers to mate within her territorial bounds. Territory is marked by the cat rubbing objects that surround it. Cats have abundant scent glands on their tail and on either side of their head. When they glance objects with these anatomical parts, they are most always deliberately or instinctively marking their territory.

That males engage in combat in a territory that is not theirs and that the female makes no sign of deterrence to the males' entering her territory is a peculiarity of the sexual state of cathood. Toms learn to battle as they mature. Almost always the tom has established his territory before he is of the age to mate. Achieving this territory likely involved either contesting with another cat or protest by a spiteful neighbor. What is learned by toms in the ritualistic rough-and-tumbles that are undertaken with other males is carried onto the fields of mating battle, where all fighting skills and trickeries are applied with passionate intensity. Whereas late-night territorial bouts (which are often chosen by the cats) rarely end in injury, the mating-right battles, to which the cats are led instinctively, may easily result in harm.

Domestic on the prowl. The cat's territory usually consists of two distinct areas: one which is absolute, defended proudly, and forms the prime hunting ground; and another, more loosely guarded, in which other cats may or may not be tolerated on their encroachment.

If successful in winning the award of the queen, whether by duel or by breeder selection, males reportedly perform with individualistic style, each having a characteristic mount, period of intromission, and response to ejaculation and the female's post-coital behavior. Additionally, each female can differentiate between males, and both males and females modify their sexual style in accordance with the others.

SOCIAL STRUCTURE AND SEX

Hierarchy is not as defined in cats as it is in many other animals. Though territorial, cats tend to fight less for territory than is commonly expected. Additionally, dominance is believed to be more random and more subject to change than is traditionally accepted. Studies indicate that dominance does not necessarily correlate to physical size, sex, or intelligence. Studies also indicate that an undiminished dominant cat in any given territory may have its place re-

Female cats assume motherhood instinctively. This domineering queen transports her strayed kitten back to the nest.

Lions, more so than any other cat, form definite, structured groups or prides, in which roles and the hierarchy of social status are clearly defined. The warmth and smell of mom ensures these cubs' security.

moved by another cat which was once his subordinate and which shows no perceivable signs of increased physical or intellectual ability. Additionally, the established hierarchy tends to be less rigidly structured than might be imagined. In many cases there is one dominant cat, but all others seemingly share an equal rank in the colony. The dominant cat apparently is less frequently challenged in battle than are subordinates by other subordinates. Very often, the dominant one uncontestedly either allows the others to partake in his shares or keeps them to himself. Additionally, subordinates are not commonly forced into absolute subjugation. Subordinates within the general vicinity live with a large degree of individuality. These findings by animal behaviorists reveal that cats may not (and perhaps cannot) develop the typical hierarchy structure that most social animals do instinctively. And this concept, if true, beams elucidation upon the tom's daily life and the grand metamorphosis that he experiences with the beckoning call of a queen that is ready to mate.

Preserving the royal line, breeders must arrange the proper pairing of the fittest and finest cats. This Persian could settle for no less.

THE KING AND QUEEN

Assuming the breed that you wish to breed is chosen, your essential concern is breeding with only the the finest possible stock. For the novice breeder who does not already own an outstanding champion stud, the recommended way to embark on breeding is to purchase the finest quality mature queen with the most solid, unflawed ancestry.

The reason for choosing the mature queen over the immature one is that with the mature female there is no chance of undesirable visible characteristics appearing in her. A desirable ancestry might include completely champion studs and any one queen having no greater than two weaknesses. While no breeder queen should be lacking in many points, it is highly likely that she will be less than perfect in some.

The tom should be an excellent all-around representative of the breed, but should especially not be deficient in any of the qualities that the queen is, and vice versa. The tom should have proven his quality with his attainment of champion status in a major breed organization. Ideally, he should also have sired champions to his credit. The purchase of such a male would necessarily be costly, and the making of one would be both costly and time consuming.

The reason, therefore, that the novice breeder is recommended to begin with a female is that it is generally less costly and more reliable to begin with a solid female and pay for the services of an outstanding stud, known as a stud fee. A stud fee is paid to the owner of the stud cat for use of the stud to sire a litter. The cost can vary in accordance with the quality of the stud, his proven record of performance, the relative rarity of the breed, and numerous other factors. It is not uncommon for a stud fee to include the right of the owner of the stud to have a pick of the litter, but the order of pick is, of course, negotiable. If you seek the services of a stud, three likely places where information can be had are local or national breed clubs and local, national or international cat-fancy periodicals.

The stud fee you pay or receive for the services of a stud varies in accordance with the quality and proven ability of the stud, the availability of good studs, and many other factors. Colorpoint Shorthair, owned by Irene B. Brounstein.

The blue gene in cat coats is recessive, which requires that a cat be homozygous for blue to exhibit the blue coloration: two blue cats will invariably produce blue kittens, though the exact shade of blue can vary. British Shorthair, blue, owned by Marcella and Ronald Syminiuk.

A hybrid breed renowned for the overall roundness of its head, the Exotic Shorthair represents the unintentional result of Persian to American Shorthair crosses.

Prepotency has some unproven truth to it as a concept; it should not, however, ever be relied upon to produce quality kittens, and it is certainly not a sound way to begin or continue a quality line of breeding stock. Prepotency refers to the tom's ability to overcome any of the queen's shortcomings. That the tom proves his superiority as a specimen in siring progeny equal or superior to his own quality holds largely true in first-generation offspring only. Therefore, to rely on only a superior stud (electing to use an inferior quality queen) to establish a breeding colony or breeding stock is a risky venture that is recommended to no one. Breed only the best possible queen to the best possible tom and your breeding program stands greater chance of producing kitten that you will be proud to call your own.

The term "superior," when used to describe the suitability of the queen and/or tom for breeding purposes, does not necessarily (and certainly not exclusively) refer to the physical characteristics exhibited by the queen and/or tom. Consideration of the breeder cat's ancestors, tracing back at least four generations, is vital to the ultimate success of all responsible breeding programs. Genes are carried in pairs, one contributed from each parent. Genes can be dominant or recessive. A dominant gene will mask the characteristics called for by the recessive gene. A cat, male or female, can therefore carry genes for faults or undesirable characteristics of the breed while showing no outward physical sign of the defect. Checking the ancestry of both cats enables the breeder to guard against undesirable traits appearing in future generations of offspring. Responsible breeder consensus holds that the average quality parent with an above-average family history is the superior choice breeder over the above-average parent with only an average to below-average lineage. Genetics and responsible breeding are inseparable concepts. It behooves the reader, whether a potential owner or breeder, to read texts that focus and specialize on genetics and breeding.

The Oriental Shorthair, like so many other breeds today, is the result of mutations which occurred within another breed, which in the Oriental's case was the Siamese. Oriental Shorthair, silver-ticked tabby, owned by Mary Minium.

Odd-eyed white Exotic Shorthair. The Exotic Shorthair is a hybrid, which means that it is the result of a breeding practice called crossbreeding, the practice of mating two cats of different breeds.

SYSTEMS

To achieve long-term success, a sound breeding program relies not only on the selection of the best possible queen and tom but also on consideration of the various methods with which breeding is conducted. Several definitions are in order.

Inbreeding refers to the practice of mating either parent to their first generation offspring or brother cats to sister cats. This method of breeding is best left to experienced professionals. It is employed to perpetuate specific desirable characteristics in concentrated form—for example, a specific tail feathering, or ear fold. Inbreeding, while often accomplishing this task, opens many doors to potential complications. Just as desirable traits are intensified, so too are negative or undesirable ones. Inbreeding should never be conducted at a greater rate than every other (alternate) mating.

Linebreeding refers to the practice of breeding related cats, often cousins, which are not as closely related as those employed in inbreeding. Linebreeding is probably the most common breeding method among professional breeders. One often hears of a specific line of a given breed as being outstanding or otherwise qualified. Linebreeding is successful because it allows the breeder to concentrate on given desirable characteristics while at the same time allowing for undesirable traits to be bred out. Though the end result, consistently outstanding progeny, may take more time than in inbreeding, the result is more solid, more long lasting, and overall better insured against catastrophe (the production of highly undesirable offspring and irreparable damage to the cattery).

Outbreeding refers to the mating of unrelated or distantly related cats of the same breed. It is usually conducted to eliminate certain undesirable characteristics from a line. It is also, however, used to infuse desirable characteristics. Outbreeding is relatively common in the cat world, but the breeder must pay great attention to the ancestry of the cat which is outbred, as the last thing any breeder wants is new undesirables appearing in the line.

Crossbreeding refers to the practice of crossing members of two different breeds. Crossbreeding is usually employed in the attempted creation of new breeds, but it is also used to add such qualities as substance or hardiness to breeds that lack them. Crossbreeding is also employed when a given breed lacks the necessary breed base to guarantee survival. Like inbreeding, crossbreeding should be used only by experienced professional breeders with a specific intention and a good knowledge of genetics. Unlike inbreeding, however, with its usually short-term and quick results, crossbreeding usually requires many generations of meticulous breeding efforts to achieve the desired ends.

Grade breeding refers to the practice of mating a purebred cat with a mongrel. It is usually employed to add such qualities as mass or vitality to a given breed lacking such. A major setback of this type of breeding is that the ancestry of the mongrel is nearly impossible to ascertain in any useful form, and undesirable characteristics can easily appear in the line.

The Singapura was first recognized in the United States in 1988 in one coat color, an ivory ground ticked with brown. In recent years, however, breeders have been selecting for additional colors naturally exhibited by the breed. Owners, Tord and Suzanne Svenson.

Cream Persian photographed in June 1984. Persians, though not the most prolific breeders, generally encounter little difficulty in birthing, as is consistent with the domesitic feline in general.

PREGNANCY

Pregnancy is a time of great change in the female. Gestation, a term that refers to the period during which the female is pregnant, typically lasts between 63 and 70 days in the domestic cat. The length of gestation, as an average, is 65 days. A litter that is carried less than 60 days will likely result in stillbirths, kittens born without life. Additionally, litters carried more than 70 days stand little chance for survival. Of course, litters have been born on the 59th or 71st day of gestation that resulted in perfectly normal cats. These figures are given only to provide the breeder-owner with a general idea regarding the length of domestic feline gestation and the consequences often faced with premature or late births.

In general, females in good health pose few breeding problems. The breeder-owner must play the essential role of nutrition provider. Feeding a sound diet contributes immeasurably to a problem-free delivery. Before mating, if possible, the female should receive a veterinary check-up, be cleared of any skin problems, checked thoroughly for the presence of parasites, and provided with a diet high in protein, vitamins, and minerals. Included in the veterinary check-up should be a stool sample that is checked for the presence of worms, as ascarids and hookworms can be transmitted to the fetuses. Any worming necessary is best performed before the second week of pregnancy, when the fetuses are at lesser risk of complications from worming procedures.

The first physical sign that the female has conceived is an increasing pinkish tone taken on by the nipples. This affects first-time mothers especially and occurs approximately 20 to 22 days after

Before serving as either sire or dam, the cat should have a thorough veterinary check-up to ensure its good health and soundness as breeding stock, even if it visibly demonstrates all the beauty of this Persian.

mating or conception. (The act of mating, or intercourse, stimulates the release of the egg. For various reasons, fertilization of the released egg may be delayed up to 24 hours. Considering these time numbers as flexible is therefore necessary.) Of course, behavioral signs may appear sooner. Though all queens do not experience a change in their behavior, common changes do include increased cleanliness (time spent grooming), a general mellowing of temperament, no interest in toms, and more time spent and desired in or very near the home. Sometime between the first and second weeks of pregnancy, the fertilized eggs, at this stage known as embryos, are implanted in the uterus. If the embryos are planted anywhere other than in the uterus, the chances of miscarriage are extremely high. If all progresses normally, sometime shortly during the third week of gestation, pregnancy can be diagnosed with a palpation check by a veterinarian. At this time an increase in the queen's food intake can be noted. Feed the queen well, but take care not to

Abyssinian kittens relish the first weeks of life, time spent in close proximity with littermates. Owner, Jaanus Cattery

Richard H. Gebhardt of the Cat Fanciers' Association shows the proper way to handle a cat. American Wirehair complying to the demonstration.

overfeed her. As her pregnancy progresses, the litter will exert pressure on the digestive system. Her meals will necessarily become smaller in net size and should be provided more frequently.

By the fifth week of gestation, the embryos, which started at the size of a single egg cell, can now be about one inch (2.5 cm). At this time, swelling to the female's abdominal region can be perceived visibly and tactilely. (Note: if the litter is particularly small, one or two kits, the female may not show visible signs of swelling until late in the pregnancy.) Necessarily, the queen will gain weight at this time and will continue to do so throughout the duration of

Prize-winning white Longhair displaying the pride and self-reliance expected of a glorious feline. The cat's outer appearance, known as its phenotype, does not necessarily predict the appearance of its offspring.

the pregnancy, the rate depending to a large degree on the number of kittens that she is carrying. Providing a sound diet at this stage is vital. Whereas we say for humans that "she is eating for two," with cats she may be eating for four or five, though at most she will consume about twice her normal rations. Important are generous amounts of easily digestible proteins, vitamins and minerals, especially calcium, as both the developing kittens and the lactation process drain the female of this vital mineral. Calcium supplements help to guard against the postnatal condition known as eclampsia, which is common to undernourished mothers.

By the seventh week of gestation, the kittens are showing considerable formation. Their heads and bodies may be discernible to the discerning veterinarian by palpation, and their skeletal frames can be seen by radiography. The activity level of the female may decrease noticeably at this time, which is normal. She should be allowed to bask, lie, and sleep as she desires. Forced exercise is not recommended, but neither is curtailing her exercising if she so chooses.

By the eighth week, the mammary glands or breasts will enlarge considerably. (By this time the female may be consuming twice her non-pregnancy rations.)

Gone are the days of placidness, if there ever were any, as sometime during the eighth or ninth week of pregnancy the queen becomes increasingly restless. She will search for a nest, a place to her liking where she can deliver her litter. By this time the owner should have on hand his own chosen box in which he wishes her to have her litter. The queen should be introduced to the box and allowed to adjust it to her liking. Additionally, she should be kept indoors at this time, and a close, though not anxious, watch should be posted. Exercise essentially should be stopped by this time, having tapered to this point gradually over the past week or so.

With the turn of the 60th day, and birth imminent, the veterinarian should be notified. If any signs of complications appear now or at birth, do not hesitate to contact the veterinarian. Commonly, the female will lose her appetite about 24 hours prior to delivery; a one-degree drop in her body temperature is also a common sign which can be observed.

Blue-cream Longhair mother with cream Longhair and blue Longhair kittens. For the first few weeks of their lives, kittens receive almost all their needs from the queen, who nurses, cleans, and warms the litter.

BIRTHING

As mentioned, preparing for the birthing process entails having a kittening box ready well in advance of the litter's birth and having the queen introduced and acclimated to the box about ten days prior to expected delivery. If she seems unwilling to take to the box,

Cornish Rex caring for her newborn kittens. Note the wire crate enclosure and the cloth bedding provided by the owner for the safety of the newborns.

first try moving it to several new locations; if this fails, then it may be best to purchase or construct a safe enclosure that will cover the box and keep the queen safely within or, if it seems reasonable (regarding safety), then simply spreading clean cloth or paper in her chosen site may be the answer. Maintaining a birthing site is essential to preventing the queen from delivering the litter in a place unbeknownst to the owner. She may suffer complications during delivery and/or a kitten or kittens may need the owner's or veterinarian's assistance. The reason that she should be introduced to the box prior to the urgency of birth is twofold: the exact date of delivery cannot be predicted without error, and the queen commonly experiences intense maternal instincts during the final days of pregnancy. She may therefore be less open to suggestion during her final days, and owner-cat conflict will be the result.

Besides the box, other useful items include: a heat lamp that can be suspended about 3.5 feet (75 cm) above the kittening box; a pair of blunt-tipped, not-very-sharp, sterile scissors to cut the umbilical cord; surgical gloves for sanitary purposes; cotton to blot clean a kitten or the mother; eyedropper; rectal and regular thermometer, one to check body temperatures and one to regulate the temperature of the kittening box; rubber tubing with syringe attached to clear a kitten of mucus, if necessary; heating pad and/or hot-water bottle to keep all warm; abundant cloth or paper to keep the box floor clean; a kitten-feeding bottle should a kitten for any reason not be able to nurse; and a scale on which to weigh the kittens.

On the average, the birthing process takes from two to three hours in normal deliveries. These figures are again rough averages only; many deliveries take four to five hours, and yet others take

The female takes so naturally to motherhood that breeder interference rarely proves necessary during the early stages of rearing, which is one reason why cats have survived so successfully in the wild.

seven to eight hours. In general, however, if the queen begins labor, which is marked by active contractions and an active attempt by the queen to expel the litter, and no kitten is delivered in one hour, a veterinarian should be consulted. The kitten may be too large or lodged in an undeliverable position. Failed or prolonged expulsion runs risk both to the queen and the rest of the litter, not to mention the kitten. This one-hour interval also holds true for each kitten born: if the duration between kittens exceeds one hour, consult a veterinarian.

At the onset of labor, provided no sign of distress is present, the female should be undisturbed in her kittening box. She will typically be restless and continuously scratch and paw the bedding in an attempt to get more comfortable. What is happening inside her at this time is that the kittens are being prepared by involuntary muscular force for entry into the birth canal and, in turn, the world. Also at this time the cervix will begin to dilate in preparation for delivery. This first stage, not considered active birthing or labor, can last up to 24 hours, though less is more common. Soon mild contractions occur with long intervals between them. During each contraction the queen will pant and often will move around. This marks the beginning of active labor, and now is the time that the queen can assist in the birthing process, for the kittens have entered or are very near the birth canal, and the queen's "bearing down" helps force

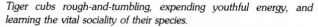

Tiger cubs rough-and-tumbling, expending youthful energy, and learning the vital sociality of their species.

Black and white bicolored mother with her very similarly colored kittens. Provided that there are no complications during birthing, the queen will soon be up and around.

the kittens along their path. Soon the contractions increase both in intensity and frequency. The queen should be reassured and kept calm. The period of increased contractions generally lasts about 30 minutes. If, however, no kitten is born within about 45 minutes, a veterinarian should be contacted. During this stage the queen strains with the contractions and continuously licks at her vulva. A liquid discharge from the vaginal region is common, as is a small amount of blood. The contractions then become very frequent and intense; delivery is imminent. A dark, thick viscous fluid will exit the vagina; within this mass, known as the amniotic sac, will be the first-born kitten of the litter. The sac may burst upon exit or may require the assistance of the queen. In either event, it is imperative that the queen take the newborn into her care, removing the entire sac and stimulating the kitten's breath.

The umbilical cord joins the kitten to the placenta. The queen should sever the cord with her teeth. The placenta will either be delivered with the kitten or shortly after. The queen may eat the placenta, and she should be allowed to do so. The placenta was attached to the wall of the uterus and served as the medium through which the kitten's nourishment passed. It is highly nutritious and is believed to stimulate the queen's production of milk. The breeder must check carefully that after each kitten follows a placenta, for a retained placenta can cause severe infection. If the queen fails to sever the umbilical cord, the breeder must intervene and cut the cord. Using too sharp a pair of scissors can lead to infection, because too clean a cut does not heal as easily. The cord should first be tied at the kitten's side of the cut. The cut cord can be blotted with iodine or another antiseptic. Some bleeding is inevitable.

Once breathing and safe, the kitten should then be placed at a teat to receive its first meal of milk, which provides the kitten with colostrum, which gives the kitten essential antibodies. If for any reason, and it sometimes will happen, the queen does not come to the assistance of the kitten, the breeder must intervene, removing the sac and stimulating the kitten's breath himself and then placing the kitten at the teats so it can feed.

Two potential problems of which the breeder must be aware are a kitten's inability to breathe and inability to feed. If mucus or other matter congests the kitten's breathing, carefully employing the syringe and tubing can bring breath to the kitten (if the breeder is a novice, he should have an experienced breeder or veterinarian supervise this activity.) If no mucus is present, simple brisk toweling, or holding the kitten face down and stroking from rear to fore, should stimulate breathing. If the kitten cannot feed, a nursing bottle must be employed. Keeping the kittens warm, about 100°F (38°C), from birth is vital. The heat lamp or hot-water bottle now proves most helpful.

Each birth should be considered as an entity unto itself, each occurring in a fashion similar to the already described process. Domestic litter sizes range from one to eight kittens, with three to five being most common. The queen has four pairs of teats, making litters greater than eight difficult for the queen to handle. In general,

Aiming for perfection. Champion Somali, bred by Carol Harrison and owned by Gale Taylor.

large litters (greater than five kittens) require supplementary feeding from a nursing bottle.

Approximately one-third of all domestic kittens are born in a feet-first position, distinguished from the breech position in that the feet are not pointing towards the head. Queens generally have little problem with delivering kittens in either the breech or the feet-first position, and mention is made only to ease the mind of the novice breeder.

Although a one-hour interval between births is normal not too uncommon is the queen's ceasing delivery for up to 24 hours, with few ill effects to either herself or her litter. A veterinarian must be contacted, however, and the queen must be watched carefully for signs of stress and distress.

Young Scottish Fold exhibiting the health and alertness expected of a well-bred kitten. All Fold kittens are born with normal-appearing ears; by four weeks of age, the fold may appear.

After delivery is complete, a veterinarian should come to view the queen and her litter. All afterbirths should be accounted for, and the vet may prescribe a shot that will ensure that no afterbirths or kittens have been retained. Once all is OK, the queen should be left to the care of the kittens. She may first wish to take a stretch and relieve herself. She should have fluids (broth, milk, and/or water) made available in case she needs a drink. She may, however, choose simply to remain by the sides of her kittens. In any case, the queen should be allowed to do as she pleases.

It is recommended that all kittens be weighed shortly after birth and that their weights be carefully monitored. A small decrease in weight for the first day or two is not cause for panic, but each kitten should soon begin to gain weight. Weight loss in kittens is commonly the first sign of an ill condition.

The breeder monitors the weight of its young charge from birth until placement into the new home. Lilac-point Balinese kitten, bred by Carol Board and owned by Carolyn Jennings.

CARING FOR THE KITTENS

Newborn kittens are very delicate and completely dependent creatures. They cannot see or hear, and their movement is very restricted. For the first week or so of their lives, kittens cannot support themselves with their legs. They move with a crawling or swimming action. They can stray from the mother and her warmth, and attention must be paid so that the kittens do not stray too far.

For the first two to three days, the kittens should be handled no more than is absolutely necessary. Under normal circumstances, the kittens will receive all their nourishment from the queen. It is therefore imperative that the mother continue to be provided with a very sound, highly nutritious diet. She may refrain from eating for the first 12 hours after delivery, but her appetite should be quickly renewed; if not, consult a veterinarian.

The newborns receive their cleanings from the mother, who will wash them with great consistency. She will also stimulate their defe-

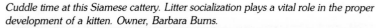

Cuddle time at this Siamese cattery. Litter socialization plays a vital role in the proper development of a kitten. Owner, Barbara Burns.

This Bengal kitten, owned by Gene Johnson of Gogees Cattery, gets some early morning exercise.

cation by lapping their bellies and vents. As was mentioned, large litters (more than five) often require supplementary bottle feeding. A commercial kitten's milk preparation should be acquired prior to delivery to have on hand just in case it is needed. In large litters, supplementary bottle feeding should be employed at alternate feedings, alternating the bottle-receiving kittens as well. Even newborn kittens will cry when hungry. Chronic crying from hunger is a cue to the breeder that supplementary feeding may be required. Monitor each kitten to see that each is receiving an adequate supply of milk; rotating the kittens to different nipples at each feeding helps

A Manx kitten at a few weeks old relies heavily upon its mother. If orphaned at a young age, the kitten will require hand-rearing.

to ensure this. Kittens that do not receive adequate milk cry, lose weight, and quickly become dehydrated. To check dehydration, one can gently pinch the skin of a kitten; if the skin does not return to its normal position when released, there is a good chance that it is dehydrated. The teats must also be regularly checked for signs of infection, which includes swelling, pus, and discoloration. If infection is present, the kittens must be bottlefed until the infection is cleared.

Few problems generally arise with bottlefeeding. Kittens have a natural instinct to suck and will typically drink readily from either a kitten nursing bottle or an eyedropper (when very young). The quantity that a young kitten will intake varies considerably from kitten to kitten but is considerably small. One key to bottlefeeding is providing frequent small meals. At each feeding the kitten should be allowed to consume its fill, and these feedings should be provided about five times a day at regular intervals.

As the kitten grows, it will consume more at each feeding, and the interval between feedings can grow, making the daily meals decrease from five to four to three, at which time the kittens are generally weaned to solid foods. An important note with bottlefeeding is that often the breeder must also stimulate the kittens to defecate, as would the mother cat. Doing so involves little more than gently stroking the kitten's abdominal and anal regions with a sterile cotton ball.

The kitten's eyes generally open sometime around the eighth day of life, but this varies considerably from litter to litter and from kitten to kitten. Eye color is typically not determinable until three months of age, but this varies considerably from breed to breed. The first teeth, known as milk teeth, cut through the kitten's gums quickly, and the second or permanent teeth are typically fully formed by the third or fourth month of life. By three weeks kittens can stand on all fours and walk, though shakily. By five weeks the kittens will commonly be clambering about the home with nimbleness and dexterity. Four to five weeks also marks the point at which weaning is begun.

These Siamese kittens, owned by Marge Naples, are just about ready to enter their new homes. Before leaving the cattery, they will be checked by a veterinarian to ensure sound health.

Under normal circumstances, the mother will commence the weaning process with an increased hesitancy to nurse the kittens. She will reduce the number of feedings and spend increasingly more time away from the litter. Often she will begin bringing solid foods to the litter herself, and it is not unheard of that the queen will bring a slayed mouse or other catch for the young kittens. To assist in the weaning process, the breeder should make soft foods regularly available to the kittens. This food can be either commercially prepared or homemade, provided that it is easily digestible

Calico Persian kitten. Calico, tricolor, and tortie each refer to three-color coat patterns. Each pattern bears uniqueness that makes it possible to classify into its respective category.

The maternal instinct of some cats is irrepressible. An unprotesting Golden Retriever bitch obliges the motherly and guard-cat impulse of the family Birman.

and nutritionally sound. After one to two weeks of the mother's weaning the kits, they should be completely weaned and eating prepared foods on their own, and the queen's lactation process should come to an end.

Housebreaking the kittens is essentially an easy process. Cats are clean animals and will quickly learn to use the litter box. Housebreaking should begin at about the same time as the weaning process. At this time the litter box should be placed inside the kittening box. If the queen also uses the box, this should help the kittens learn the appropriate behavior, but in any event kittens typically prove quick learners. A helpful tip is that using a different medium to line the litter box from that used to line the kittening box helps the kittens to distinguish the boxes and learn where to go. By the sixth to eighth week of age, the kittens are typically weaned and litter-box trained and prepared to leave for their new homes.

GENETICS

Genetics is the study of how traits and characteristics are passed from parent to offspring. Genetics has been practiced in the scientific world since the time of Mendel and his observation of peas. For a time it was questioned and even ridiculed, but like so many scientific hypotheses, genetics has come to be an integral part of modern life. The breeding of domestic animals was once based on common-sense experimentation and tried-and-true traditional methods of producing desired offspring. Without ever having heard the word genetics, breeders in many cases actually practiced in basic form many of the proven-correct laws of genetics as they apply to breeding. However, both the experimentors and conservative breeders had to deal with a considerable margin of error and numerous undesirable stock.

Today, with genetic principles so easily accessible to the general public, most every (if not all) responsible and successful breeding program is based solidly on sound genetic laws and rules. By employing genetics, the breeder can look beyond the visible characteristics (the phenotype) of the cat, to the cat's genotype, the traits

Whether these two pedestal-sitting Himalayans could produce similarly attractive off-spring can only be determined by considering their genotypes.

A family of Shorthair kittens. Note the remarkable consistency of type and markings expressed by the offspring. Sound, reliable breeding rests firmly on sound genetic knowledge and practice.

that it carries in a recessive state, hidden—traits that can and likely will appear in the breeding line should genetic principles not be employed.

The world of domestic cat breeds is truly a diversified, highly detailed microcosm. Taillessness, folded ears, curl ears, and hairlessness refer to but a few of the more outstanding traits exhibited by today's breeds, with myriads more, many subtle, underlining essential characteristics. Without complete comprehension of all characteristics and traits and the way in which they are passed genetically, the breeder today is completely in the dark, breeding irresponsibly.

Of course, it is beyond the scope of this breed handbook to discuss genetics in detail. The owner who is considering breeding is strongly encouraged to undertake a study of genetics before embarking on such a responsibility-entailing adventure.

RESPONSIBILITY

Breeders have come a long way in recent years. Today some of the finest specimens of domestic cat are seen at shows, in homes, and on the silver screen. With ever-increasing knowledge—biological, psychological, and ecological—we human beings propagate the domestic feline. Yet, vital concerns remain, sometimes unaddressed, and often overlooked. The breeding of cats can be a rewarding, enjoyable, and beneficial experience—no one will deny that. But the breeding of cats, when conducted wantonly, irresponsibly, can also be a miserable, cruel, disastrous experience. Thousands upon thousands of cats and kittens are put to cold death every year for lack of homes, lack of funds, and lack of breeder responsibility. Many of these unfortunate innocents suffer because of genetic malconditions and malformation. Many others are orphans, the consequence of owners not spaying their roaming charges. The breeding of cats must be conducted only by knowledgeable, good-intentioned persons. Breeding is costly. It typically does not reap financial rewards. Breeding is toilsome. It requires many hours and strong dedication. Breeding is difficult. It demands commitment, concern, abundant virtue and an absence of vice.

Opposite: The hairless quality of the Sphynx breed results from a mutant recessive gene. Because of its recessiveness, this gene can be carried for generations by seemingly normal-coated cats. **Below:** *The marcel coat of the Cornish Rex also results from a mutation—the rex gene mutations are located at a different loci than are the genes for normal coat.*

Unbridled Felinity—
the
Wild
Cats

Felis sylvestris, *the European wild cat.*

African Golden Cat

Felis aurata

Portrait Twice the size of any apartment-dwelling feline, the golden cat of Africa displays more than golden coloration: occurring in many shades of brown, red and gray; fawn and slate gray are the parameters of the spectrum. Shading and spotting are both common. The coat is short and dense. The small head rests on a sturdy body; the backs of the ears are typically black in color. The legs are fairly lengthy, and the tail is moderately long (about a foot), with bands sometimes apparent. In height the golden cat stands 20 inches (50 cm) high; the length is 35 inches (91 cm), although the average is probably five inches less. Weight: 34 pounds (15 kg).

Distribution A most infrequently sighted wild cat whose range seems to extend through the mountain and deciduous forest regions of central and western Africa.

Behavior Resourceful and secretive, as African natives relate, the golden cat hunts during twilight and/or dusk and is known to be active at night. Besides easily accessible insects and birds, the golden cat is fierce enough to conquer small forest dwellers such as duikers (small horned antelopes); pygmy antelopes; and water chevrotains (small, hornless, deerlike animals).

n.b. Pygmy tribes in Cameroon consider the tail of the golden cat to be a symbol of good fortune, especially on an elephant hunt. Other tribesmen regard the pelt as too valuable to trade and remain reticent about their sources.

215

African Wild Cat

Felis libyca

Portrait To a fair degree resembling the domestic cat, the African wild cat is larger and more solid in build than its oft-cited descendant. The head and body average 23 inches (58.5 cm) in length, while height at the shoulder is typically 14 inches (35.5 cm). Weight: about 12 pounds (5.4 kg). The tail is usually long, thin and tapered, with a black tip and several distinct rings. Coloration varies with the specimen; two types as distinctly different as grayish tan and iron gray are reported to exist in the same general vicinity, with an innumerous variety of shades in between. Markings on the face are tabbylike; spots on the chest and other foreparts; stripes extend the length of the spine; and the upper limbs are encircled by bands.

Distribution The African wild cat ranges throughout the African continent, excepting the dense inner area of the equatorial belt and the intensely dry deserts. Closely resemblant species can be found north to Sicily, Morocco and Algeria.

Behavior Highly adaptable, the African wild cat is said to survive on almost any terrain: whether in forest, plain, mountain, or bush, this solitary cat makes feast on small mammals and rodents, reptiles, birds, and insects. The African wild cat houses the power and determination to slay small antelope. It is nocturnal in habit and very seclusive and aloof, though not too shy of man to seek abode near his towns.

n.b. *The gestation period of the African wild cat is between 56–60 days, which makes it closer to the domestic cat than to the European wild cat.*

Felis badia

Bay Cat

Portrait   One color characteristic that distinguishes the bay cat from other cats of the East Indies is the paucity of dark spots and stripes (faint stripes can occur on the face and cheeks). The backs of the ears are typically black with distinctive white markings; this color patch also occurs on the ground side of the tail tip. The overall coloration is described as yellowish to chestnut brown, often with a reddish hue, and fading to a lighter shade on the underbody. The tail is long and tapering. Slightly larger than the domestic cat, the bay cat in general appearance resembles a small Temminck's cat. Head to tail: average 21 inches (53 cm). Tail: 21.5 inches (55 cm).

Distribution   Quite rare, the bay cat, also known as the Bornean red cat, is native exclusively to the island of Borneo. Reports vary, but it is believed that the bay cat prefers densely grown forests and often roams high altitudes, 2950 feet (900 m).

Behavior   Early studies relied almost exclusively on the dissecting of long dead (often inadequate) specimens, and what scientists ascertained of the bay cat's behavior was based mostly on reports made to them by hunters and natives who observed the cats in the wild. When first described by Gray in 1874, the bay cat was placed as the sole member of the genus named *Badiofelis*, which was later renamed to *Profelis*.

n.b.   *Feasting on small mammals, the bay cat has two less than endearing proclivities, offal eating and viciousness.*

Black-footed Cat

Felis nigripes

Portrait   Known as the world's smallest wild feline, the black-footed cat is indeed smaller than most domestic cat breeds. Average length is about 16 inches (40.5 cm) and weight averages at 4 pounds (1.8 kg). Head broad, with small ears colored black on their outer side and marked with a white splash. Tail averages at a short 7 inches (18 cm); it tapers to the black tip and is marked with incomplete black bars. A desert dweller, the black-footed cat boldly sports rows of round dark spots on its coat of sandy brown.

Distribution   Widely distributed, though scarcely populous throughout southern, southeast and southwest Africa, through the Kalahari desert and preferring the arid, desert climes.

Behavior   A master of deceit, the crevice-creeping black-footed cat enters unseen the burrows of small earth-dwelling animals to await quietly their return. Nocturnal and seclusive, the *Sebulabulakwana,* as the black-foot is known in its native land, reportedly overcomes any shortcomings in size with its intense ferocity. Believably feeding on small mammals, rodents, birds, and reptiles, the black-footed cat can conquer many animals that are four times its own size. Though relatively little is known about its breeding habits, black-footed cats usually rear their litters of two or three kits in underground burrows. Specimens have been kept and bred in captivity, though infrequently.

n.b.   *Imagination and/or intentional fabrication—or truth: African inhabitants report that the black-footed cat clings to the neck of a mystified giraffe, gouging its neck until the jugular is severed and the feline has a feast for a king (or tribal chief).*

218

Bobcat

Felis rufus

John R. Quinn '90

Portrait   Closely related to and resembling the lynx, the bobcat, also called the bay lynx and American wild cat, is smaller than the Canadian lynx, with thinner, smaller feet and less-tufted ears. Coat color ranges from yellow-brown through various shades of buff to gray; most commonly the bobcat is spotted and lined with black to blackish brown, with a black streak on its crown. Height averages 21 inches (53 cm). Weight is typically no greater than 32 pounds (14.5 kg), though the species varies considerably with geographic location. The bobcat's voice is distinctive in its range, at times suggestive of a "coughlike bark."

Distribution   Ranging from the far northern U.S., into British Columbia and Nova Scotia, and south to Mexico, the bobcat inhabits widely varying terrain and is the most numerous of the North American wild cats. Extermination methods in the eastern and midwestern U.S. have prohibited the bobcat from this section of its native territory.

Behavior   The bobcat is bold and highly adaptable: it prefers seclusion and the solid earth, but will take to the trees with ease when pursued by a predator or when pursuing prey; it will not retreat from the advancing steps of civilization. The bobcat's home is a den, which it locates in a most inconspicuous cover. Marking with scent is an outstanding behavior characteristic, especially fecal marking by females with young litters. The bobcat will indulge in a swim more readily than most cats, especially if the end result is a tasty morsel; its main prey species, however, are rabbits and rodents, thus controlling very definite pests for man. The bobcat will attack domestic livestock if necessity is the force, which it oftimes is; this forced behavior has bred a bloody antagonism between man and bobcat.

n.b.   *The bobcat has two characteristics that set it apart from other cats: the bobcat plucks its prey before consuming it, and the bobcat is the only wild cat that can purr during both inhalation and exhalation.*

219

Caracal Lynx

Felis caracal

John R. Quinn '90

Portrait   True to its common name, the long-legged, tufted-eared caracal lynx bears fair resemblance to the other lynx species. Its long tail, however, is a distinguishing characteristic that once led taxonomists to classify the caracal as the sole member of the genus *Caracal*, under the name *Caracal caracal*. The coat is dense but short, with no side whiskers. Color varies in uniform shades of reddish brown, with white markings on the chin, throat, underbelly and around the eyes, which in keeping with the other lynx species contract to form circles. A thin black line runs from the nose to the eye. The ears are colored black on their outsides and are abundantly tufted with long black hairs. Length of the caracal is about 29 inches (74 cm). Typical weight is about 38 pounds (17.5 kg).

Distribution   Widely distributed throughout Africa and southern Asia. Preferring arid terrain but entering neither the depths of sand deserts nor the perimeters of the equatorial belt. The species was once especially common in South Africa.

Behavior   The caracal, known also as the desert lynx, fares best on the dry plains and "moist" deserts but is adaptable enough to survive in the wood and other terrain types, with the absolute exception of tropical and evergreen forests. Essentially the soloist in darkness, the caracal can also be seen roaming fearless in broad daylight. The species climbs superbly and, not unlike the cheetah in style, is probably the fastest feline of its general size. Remarkably, the caracal is renowned for its ability to ground birds on the wing. Reportedly breeds well in captivity.

n.b.   *The name caracal was given to the species by Buffon, who derived it from the Turkish word* karakal *meaning black ear, two of which make the caracal quickly spotted in the wild.*

Acinonyx jubatus

Cheetah

Portrait A most unique cat, the cheetah differs more from the rest of its lot than do any other two felines: long of leg and most aerodynamic, the cheetah is designed entirely for acceleration. The cheetah's divergence from the feline norm occurred ages ago (likely during the Pliocene period), and the species itself has considerably reduced its size since that time. Long and lithe, the species is characteristically darkly spotted on its coarse tawny to bright fawn coat. Height: 31 inches (79 cm). Weight: 88–157 pounds (40 to 72 kg). Head and body length: about 4 feet (120 cm).

Distribution Now extinct in India, the cheetah has a limited range throughout Africa and, in Asia, south of the Ganges and west of Bengal.

Behavior Renowned as the fastest extant land animal, cheetahs have attained 55 mph (90 kph) in captivity and 60 mph (100 kph) in the wild. Such speeds are short lived and necessitate considerable rest periods prior to their exertion. The cheetah does not stalk its prey, as do other cats, but flat out runs down, knocks over, and slays its victim. That the cheetah could be tamed was recognized by man millennia ago, reportedly as far back as 3000 BC. The Sumerians were great lovers of the sport, and Europeans, especially during the Italian Renaissance, found the pastime undeniably most civilized: cheetahs were carried on pillowed horseback to the hunting site, where they were released to slay rabbit and roe deer. Its hunting prowess and its spots earned it the alternative common name of hunting leopard. Undoubtedly the cheetah's extinction in India and low numbers worldwide are attributable to the capturing of kits and adults (which were found to be more easily trained) to serve royalty as cats of the hunt; ironically, adult cheetahs were ruthlessly hunted by these same thrill-seeking bipeds. Breeding in captivity was not achieved until the 1950s. Cheetahs do not fare well as captives: as many as 75 percent of them succumb to liver and/or kidney disorders.

n.b. *Kublai Khan reportedly kept 1000 cheetahs for hunting purposes.*

Chinese Desert Cat

Felis bieti

Portrait   This rather large yellowish gray-colored cat was first described in 1892 from pelts only. Later, when a skull was acquired, the species was found to resemble closely the jungle cat. The coat, the length of which grows considerably in preparation for the cold months, is typically darker on the back and sides, fading to a whitish gray on underside; stripes extend to the flanks, which remain unmarked. Ears are yellowish brown, adorned with short upstanding hairs at their tips. Indistinct brownish streaks typically dress the cheeks. Tail is ringed with black. Head and body length: 33 inches (85 cm). Tail length: 13.7 inches (35 cm).

Distribution   The outer borders of China, eastern Tibet, and Mongolia are the apparent lines that enclose the range of the Chinese desert cat, known also as the pale desert cat.

Behavior   Roaming the steppes and forested mountains of its native lands, the Chinese desert cat defies its name: it is not the arid-loving feline which might be assumed. Hunters convey the ferocity, agility, and hardiness of the species in their reports of dogs undone at 9000 feet (2700 m) by a single indomitable feline. Due both to the seclusive habits of the cat and unconquerable terrain that it successfully inhabits, little is actually known about the reproduction and lifestyle of this most stoic animal.

n.b.   The Chinese desert cat was given its name prematurely, before much could be ascertained about its distribution. Based on its coloration, it was assumed that the species inhabited semi-desert terrain—because of the mystery that continues to shroud the species, it is assumed that a misnomer is a suitable common name.

Panthera nebulosa   Clouded Leopard

John R. Quinn '89

Portrait About half the size of a small leopard (essentially a mid-sized wild cat), the clouded leopard shares characteristic features with both the small and large felids. Placed in the now-abandoned genus *Neofelis* in 1821 by Griffith, the clouded leopard sports a marbled coat pattern ranging from yellow to light brown, which closely resembles the coat of the marbled cat. The underbody is whitish. Two black bands mark the cheeks: one from each eye to ear; another parallel to the mouth. The skull is long and narrow. The ears small, marked black with gray patches. The upper canines achieve a relative length greater than that of any other feline. (They have been described as tusklike, resembling those of the extinct saber-toothed tiger). Tail is thick. Height: about 20 inches (50 cm). Weight: 20 pounds (9 kg). Canines: 1–2 inches (2.5–5 cm).

Distribution Southern China and IndoChina, Formosa, Borneo, Nepal and Burma.

Behavior The clouded leopard climbs trees with unchallenged mastery—only the margay approaches its ability to maneuver and descend. The species dwells in the forest, living a nocturnal, seclusive life. Natives assert that animals "sleep" in trees, specifically between forked branches, and wait for their meal to arrive, usually a large bird or other tree-dweller. The species is relatively little known, however. It has been reported that it will prey on livestock, including pigs and goats, and that European sportsmen shot most of their cats on the ground. Additionally, captive specimens have shown considerable day-time activity.

n.b. *As suggested in its Malayan name* rimau-dahan, *which loosely means tree (or forked branch) tiger, the species is renowned for its ability to slay monkeys and birds in the trees in which these prey seek shelter, so swift is the cat.*

European Wild Cat

Felis silvestris

John R. Quinn

Portrait   Believed to have crossed with innumerous domestic cats, the European wild cat is a distinctive species that is larger (about one-third), stronger, and much wilder than any domestic feline. The tail of the wild cat is shorter than the domestic's and does not taper, ending in a blunt tip. The coat color ranges in yellowish and brownish grays, with mackerel tabby markings. The undercat shades to a more yellowish hue, while the throat is typically whitish. The tail is encircled with dark marks, which turn to rings, ending in a blackish tip. Length: approximately 31.5 inches (80 cm). Tail: 13.5 inches (35 cm). Weight: 5–13 pounds (2–6 kg).

Distribution   At one time populous throughout the British Isles (possibly excluding Ireland), Europe, and extending into western Asia. Later the species was driven to near extinction throughout most of its range. Today, man's realization of the value of the species to the ecology has cast new hope for its future, though its numbers will inevitably remain low.

Behavior   Also known as the forest wild cat, the European wild cat has for centuries roamed the once vast and dense woodlands of Europe. The species is a fearless hunter of vermin. Because it prefers a seclusive life, the animal is not a popular captive species. It is believed by some that the European wild cat is the direct ancestor of some breeds of domestic cat, but one would never surmise this from its untamable, vicious nature.

n.b.   *Aside from man, the lynx poses the greatest threat to this wild cat; with acute ferocity, the wild cat slays such formidable would-be predators as the golden eagle.*

Felis viverrinus

Fishing Cat

Portrait   The species name of *viverrinus* was given to the species by Bennett in 1833 as witness to the fishing cat's physical similarity to the Asiatic civet, *Viverra zibetha*. The fishing cat is a stocky feline, weighing about 25 pounds (11.5 kg), with a large broad skull and a tail of only about one-quarter to one-third of the total body length of 33.5 inches (85 cm). A tropical dweller, the cat has small ears and carries a short, coarse coat that is typically grayish brown. Coat markings take the shape of dark spots that turn to longitudinal stripes on the neck and head. The ears are typically colored black with white central spots. The forefeet are well webbed, and the claws are not fully retractable.

Distribution   The fishing cat has a wide distribution throughout southern and southeastern Asia and can be found in Sumatra, Siam, Indochina, Taiwan, Ceylon, Nepal, and elsewhere.

Behavior   When asked to fight or flee, the fishing cat invariably chooses combat—to the death, if necessary. The species acquires its rather peculiar common name from its innate ability to hunt fish, crustaceans and mollusks with its paws. The fishing cat, not surprisingly, seems to have a natural affinity for water: reports cast the cat wading untroubled in shallow streams and uninhibitedly throwing itself into deep waters to capture its chosen prey. Natives fearfully respect the ability and strength of the 25-pound (11.5-kg) fishing cat. Statements of both natives and missionaries portray the cat in the role of childnapper: snatching months-old children from unguarded huts.

n.b.   *One captive specimen escaped from its cage to slay a leopard twice its size! However, it is regarded as a tamable species.*

Flat-headed Cat

Felis planiceps

Portrait   A most physically distinctive feline, the flat-headed cat, like the fishing cat, bears resemblance to the viverrids, but in addition shares features with the mustelids. The topskull is broad and flat, and the foreskull is pointed, overall appearing as a flat wedge. The nasal bones form an unmistakable ridge, and bone completely encircles the eye orbits. Dentition is highly modified: the upper rear molar runs two roots and is greater in size and development than in any other feline. The coat is long, soft, and thick, and varies considerably in color. The head is typically brownish red; the body blackish brown, tipped white; underbody, whitish, splashed with brown; face fair reddish, with two thin dark lines across the cheeks. Head and body: about 22 inches (56 cm). Tail: about 7 inches (18 cm).

Distribution   Found in southern Asia, Borneo, Sumatra, and Malaysia, in terrain reaching nearly a mile above sea level.

Behavior   Few facts exist about the lifestyle of this intriguing felid. It is nocturnal and has become tame in captivity, although incidents of its being captive have been minimal. Its peculiar dentition allows the flat-headed cat to seize slippery fish adroitly. It is known to catch fish, frogs, and mollusks. Reports also suggest that the flat-headed cat will feast on chickens and other small domestic animals. In terms of reproduction and family life, little is known.

n.b.   *Never the farmer's favorite, the flat-headed cat reportedly finds an occasional sweet potato or garden fruit indubitably delectable.*

Felis geoffroyi

Geoffroy's Cat

Portrait   A large, wide but short, convex skull and small anterior premolars are notably distinct features of Geoffroy's cat; they are, however, shared traits with the kodkod, making these two South American species believably closely related. The build is substantial. Head and body: 27.5 inches (70 cm). The length of the tail is about half that of the body. Coloration varies considerably with geographic location, ranging from silver in the south to brilliant ochre in the north and highlands. Small evenly sized black spots mark the coat, and several black streaks accentuate the head and cheeks. Backs of the rounded ears are black with large central white spots. Tail is spotted at its root and striped towards its tip.

Distribution   Geoffroy's cat is believed to be exclusive to central South America, but some believe that the species may extend to farther south.

Behavior   An avid tree scaler who never fears the water, Geoffroy's cat is quite the dexterous, adaptable feline. The seemingly most poignant aversion that this species has is for man: at high cost Geoffroy's cat avoids human settlements. It is known as *gato montes* (translating to mountain cat) by Argentineans, and has been known to inhabit heights in the Bolivian Andes reaching 11,500 feet (3,500 m). If given the choice, Geoffroy's cat prefers scrub-laden woodlands and bushy plains, in or on which it can lead a primarily terrestrial life, feeding on small mammals and birds. Litter size is two to three kits.

n.b.   *None too keen on crossbreeding, captive male Geoffroy's cats have been known to slaughter all domestic females introduced for breeding purposes.*

Iriomotes Cat

Felis iriomotensis

Portrait   In general size, the Iriomotes cat is about the same as the typical domestic cat. Its length, however, is greater, and its tail is comparatively shorter. Head and body: 25 inches (64 cm). Tail: 17 inches (43 cm). Its build strongly suggests its ground-hunting proclivities: short-legged and low-slung, the cat speaks of an adept hunter in dense undergrowth. The coat color ranges from dark to yellowish brown, with rows of black spots which tend to fuse into bands and about seven dark lines on the neck which extend to the shoulder. The ears are rounded; their backs are black with white central spots.

Distribution   The Iriomote island is approximately 113 square miles (181 km); it is the exclusive indigenous home of the Iriomotes cat.

Behavior   The Iriomotes cat roamed the remote island of Iriomote, situated in the south end of the Ryukyu group, about 125 miles (200 km) from Taiwan. Within this densely forested, uninvestigated terrain the cat prowled the ground in search of small rodents, birds, and other mammals. Caught occasionally in a native's boar trap, the flesh of the species holds high favor among culinary-minded Iromotians. The Iriomotes cat was not identified by scientists until 1967, but for centuries natives have known it well. Related to some extent to the leopard cat, the Iriomotes cannot trace its exact ancestry. A forest dweller, it is similar in appearance to the kodkod and Geoffroy's cat, but is doubtfully related.

n.b.   *The Iriomotes cat inhabits such a small fraction of the globe that its numbers are unquestionably small. The Japanese naturalist and writer Yukio Tagawa was one of the first non-natives to venture forth in search of the reported cat. Initially unsuccessful, Mr. Tagawa coaxed (his methods remain secret) natives into trading him a captured specimen.*

Panthera onca

Jaguar

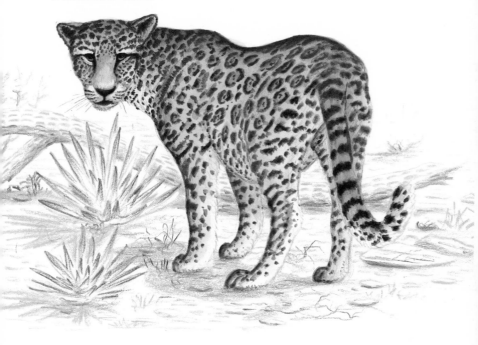

Portrait A massive cat with a distinguishing coat pattern of complete black circles on the back and flanks, with one to three central spots. The melanistic jaguar, a solid-black animal, is not uncommon in the wild or in the "tame" minds of man. Albinotic specimens are also reported. The head is large and rounded; the chest is deep, powerful and barrellike in its spring of rib. Head and body length: 73 inches (185 cm). Tail: 30 inches (74 cm). The jaguar was first reported by Amerigo Vespucci, in 1500, in Venezuela, and referred to as a leopard. It was later called a tiger, and much of the Spanish-speaking world commonly refers to the species as *el tigre*. Indeed, the jaguar rivals the tiger in its strength and awesome bearing.

Distribution Once roaming throughout North and South America, the jaguar is now extremely endangered in the U.S., and its numbers remain globally low.

Behavior Fair in trees but superb in water, jaguars hunt animals ranging from snakes to monkeys to horses to man. Once adults, jaguars have no natural predators in their native lands: man is their only threat. The jaguar stalks its prey with solemn determination, burning concentration, and patience. It is silent. The jaguar will wait in cover for its prey to arrive or lunge into strong currents, if this means success. The jaguar is known to kill such formidable foes as boas and anacondas, caiman crocodilians, and arapaima (a fresh water fish measuring up to 13 feet, 4 m, and weighing up to 450 pounds, 200 kg).

Jaguarundi

Felis yagouaroundi

Portrait   The jaguarundi is most unfeline in appearance; so much so in fact that authorities have jokingly suggested that its common name be changed to otter cat, in view of the species' seemingly lutrine skull. There are two varieties of the species: one of a very dark coloration that shades to a lighter hue on the underbelly, and a second that is reddish brown in color. Specimens of the lighter varieties are commonly called eyras, but both can appear in a single litter, and neither is considered a subspecies. With short legs, a rather long thin tail, and an elongated body, the jaguarundi appears more like a tree dweller than the ground cat that it is.

Distribution   Ranging from Arizona through Texas, south to southern Brazil and northern Argentina, the species is most common in Central and South America.

Behavior   The jaguarundi is a forest-dwelling feline that prefers thickety undergrowth and hedges and scrubby forest edges. It is most active during the early morning and late evening hours, when it prowls the ground in search of rodents, birds, and small mammals. It should not be referred to as a nocturnal creature, as jaguarundis can be spotted active during bright daylight—it is, however, partial to a noontime nap. Jaguarundis are not hesitant to enter the morsel-laden abodes of humans, and such visits are often the cat's undoing. The jaguarundi is essentially a solitary creature that can communicate with birdlike chirps and friendly purrs. Not known for its protective maternal instincts, the jaguarundi mom has been known to abandon her kits in times of danger.

n.b.   *Apparently, jaguarundis are kept as semi-domesticated pets by South American Indians to control rodent populations.*

Felis chaus

Jungle Cat

Portrait   The jungle cat sports a coloration that ranges from grayish yellow to reddish brown; all the various shades are ticked agouti. Both the legs and tail are marked with stripes. (As in various other wild cats, the jungle cat's stripe markings are clearer in kittens and immatures). The torsos of adults are typically unmarked. Small black pencil hairs adorn the ears, which are reddish in color and without white markings or bars. The legs are characteristically long, and the tail short. Its physical resemblance to the Abyssinian is often stated. Height: 13–14 inches (33–36 cm). Head to tail: 30 inches (75 cm). Tail: 13.5 inches (34 cm).

Distribution   Asia and northern Africa loosely define the jungle cat's rather extensive roaming grounds, which include   such countries as Egypt, Israel, Iran, Afghanistan, Sri Lanka (Ceylon), Burma, Thailand (Siam), and western China.

Behavior   Known also as the reed cat, the jungle cat is an adaptive abandoned-den dwelling feline found in forests, plains, and open and cultivated fields, where it prowls the ground in search of small rodents, other mammals, and birds. The jungle cat is also known to relocate in human dwellings left vacant. The jungle cat is one of two definitely feline creatures etched upon the walls of ancient Egyptian monuments. The Egyptians, known for their domesticating proclivities, believably used the cats to hunt wild fowl. The jungle cat on the hunt is a silent, slow, meticulous sportsman. It breeds well in captivity but is not a popular exhibit.

n.b.   *Quick and powerful, the jungle cat is known to be a potential predator of cheetah kits.*

Kodkod

Felis guigna

Portrait Brown to yellowish ochre color the coat, which is marked with black spots on the body, stripes on the chest, and rings on the tail. The backs of the ears are colored black, with white central spots. Melanistic specimens are not uncommon and occur in litters of normal-colored kits. A larger variety, typically colored in the kodkod's lighter range and with un-spotted feet occurs in central Chile, while smaller, more brightly colored specimens with spotted feet occur farther to the south. As is that of Geof-froy's cat, the kodkod's skull is large and wide but short and convex, and the anterior premolars, minute. The cat's closest relative, however, is the tiger cat. Having a head-to-tail length of only about 20 inches (51 cm), a tail of 8.5 inches (21–22 cm), the kodkod is probably the smallest wild cat in the Western world.

Distribution The central and southern portions of South America comprise the kodkod's hunting grounds.

Behavior Of the many feline species of which little is known about their social behavior, the kodkod ranks with the foremost of them. To this date, specialists agree on two ideas only: the kodkod dwells in the forest and it is most active at night. Much else of what has been thus far postulated re-lies on inept discussions and dubious accounts. Some scholars assert that the species is arboreal and dexterous in the boughs, while others claim that the kodkod is clumsy when climbing trees, prefers the solid ground, and is given to picking an easy chicken from an angry farmer's coop.

n.b. *That the kodkod may travel and hunt in packs has also been posed, but little other than fervent farmers' accounts attest to this claim.*

Panthera pardus **Leopard**

John P. Quinn '90

Portrait The leopard, also commonly called the panther, is found in a variety of types (some assert subspecies). This variance confused the orderly Romans, who attempted to classify the animal as two species based primarily on tail length (22 versus 28 vertebrae). In general, the leopard is grand and graceful, lean and well muscled, with massive limbs and an elongated body. The coat is short and sleek in warm and tropical climates but warm and long in cold climes. Head to tail: 60 inches (152.5 cm). Tail: 38 inches (96 cm). Weight: 90–122 pounds (41–55 kg). Color ranges from pale yellow and buff gray to brilliant ochre and chestnut. White colors the chest, throat, belly and the insides of the limbs. Black spots, blotches, and rosettes dot the coat of the cat. Black leopards, the melanistic phase, are more common in southern Asia than in tropical Africa, though they prefer moist, densely forested regions.

Distribution Ages ago found throughout Europe, including Great Britain. The leopard finds its endangered wild existence today limited to small portions of Africa and Asia. The republican Romans reaped their first leopards, used as gladiators in the ring, from North Africa, where they were once very common.

Behavior Highly adaptable, leopards are known to thrive in nearly every type of the wide range of terrains throughout Asia and Africa, with the limited exception of desert regions. So long as there is food, even if the prey be man, leopards will survive. The species has proven the most dangerous feline to man, in part due to their ophidian village entry, superb strength, and leaping and climbing proclivities. Leopards are renowned for their ability to survive in densely human-populated areas. The leopard is a stalker, a large game hunter, with excellent swimming ability.

n.b. *Once hunted without mercy for its highly stylish coat, the leopard today is an endangered species and granted full protection from the gun, the bow, and other life-ending devices.*

Leopard Cat

Felis bengalensis

John R. Quinn '90

Portrait Changing with the terrain, the leopard cat's pelage widely varies in color from yellowish ochre and brown through silver. The coat is spotted and patched with black markings, which on the head and white chest take the form of stripes. Though it stands taller, the leopard cat is generally referred to as about the size of the domestic cat. Head to rump: 24 inches (60 cm). Tail: 16 inches (40 cm), and thick. The short, rounded skull houses eye orbits with sockets open at their backs. The anterior premolars are typically present.

Distribution From southern Asia, including India, through China, Manchuria, and eastern Siberia ranges this tree-scaling, small-sized wild cat. The smaller specimens are found in the Philippine Islands, while the larger occur in the northern part of the distribution.

Behavior Among the most common of the south Asian wild felids, the leopard cat prefers the shelter of the forest and jungle; it also fares well on the mountains and on protective hills. The leopard cat dens in hollow trees, from which it emerges to pounce rodents, wild fowl and small birds, and small mammals. So graceful and agile is the species that some claim it makes the domestic cat seem awkward and ponderous.

n.b. *Leopard cats have been kept in captivity since the early 1970s; little of their innate character has changed, and they maintain their fearful reputation for ferocity. The leopard cat is the wild cat used to create the domestic-wild hybrid called the Bengal.*

Panthera leo

Lion

Portrait The largest African carnivore, the lion can weigh as much as 400–500 pounds (180–225 kg), stand three feet (90 cm) at the shoulder and be nine feet (2.7 m) in length. For the average person, a description of the lion is roaringly superfluous, as it is perhaps the single animal that has had the greatest effect on the imagination of man; its image is vivid in most minds. The face is broad, the ears round. The shortish neck is adorned by a thick mane in the male; the female goes without. The mane darkens with age from its initial yellow to a brown or reddish brown. The coat color varies substantially—from light buff to a dark ochre brown. The tail which extends 41 inches (104 cm) is ended by a black tuft. The legs and body are powerful and impressive.

Distribution The continent of Africa, south of the Sahara and in the Gir forest of India; at one time from the Cape of Good Hope to the Mediterranean, and eastward as far as northern India. Today it is more restricted to protected areas of Africa and the aforementioned Indian forest.

Behavior The only truly social cat, the lion is polygamous and protects its pride with unfaltering ability. These mythological and proverbial Africans hunt alone, in pairs and/or in bands. The zebra and the gazelle are their most easily fallen prey; giraffes and buffaloes require more effort. In general lions do not like to run and will often not chase their prey; they are among the most patient of animals and capitalize on their strength and ability to surprise an unsuspecting, preferably sleeping, herd.

235

Marbled Cat

Felis marmorata

John R. Quinz '89

Portrait Approximately the size of a very large household cat, this felid is stunningly patterned with dark blotches, each outlined in black, spewed over a brownish gray to well-lit yellow ground. Additionally the limbs are dotted with solid black ovals. The length of the head and body averages about 21 inches (53 cm); the tail, about 15 inches (38 cm). The head is much on the rounded side, more so than the average feline; the skull is broad and flat. Insulated by woolly underfur, the pelt is dense and soft. The dentition is impressive, although the premolars are scarcely prominent. The body is lengthy; the tail is bushy and long. The ears are smallish and rounded at the the tips; in color the backs of the ears are black with gray bars.

Distribution Nepal, Sikkim, Assam, Burma, Malaya, Indochina, Borneo, and Sumatra comprise the forest landscapes in which the marbled cat dwells.

Behavior Although very little is actually known of this wild cat's habits and day-to-day routine, it is believed that the marbled cat hunts principally by night, on land and in trees. Its arboreal method often has it climbing up a tree in pursuit of a feathered meal. Among its ground-dwelling meal prospectives are rats and squirrels (unless, of course, the latter ladders its way up a nearby tree); additionally, lizards and frogs may occasionally be slurped by this less-than-finicky forest felid.

n.b. *While not fussy in its choice of menu, the marbled cat is not fond of leftovers and refuses to indulge in a left-over carcass.*

Felis wiedii

Margay

John R. Quinn '90

Portrait   Higher on leg and longer in tail, the margay or marguey resembles a miniaturized ocelot, and in parts of South America it is even referred to as the "little ocelot." This cat's extensive tail (measuring nearly 20 inches, 70 cm) and also its attractive spotted pattern provide its alternative name of long-tailed spotted cat. The margay's pattern is comprised on rows of longitudinally arranged brown circular markings which grow softer in color as they approach the center; the ear backs are black with white central spots; the tail is spotted and ringed. The ground color is yellow-brown, with white markings on belly, chest, throat, chin, and limbs. The coat is soft. The eyes are prominently large. Body length: 27 inches (68 cm).

Distribution   Known in the United States but is more common further south; in South America found in Panama, northern Colombia, and Peru, as well as regions of Paraguay, Uruguay and northern Argentina.

Behavior   The tree-climbing margay is indisputably the "monkey" of the cat world: no other feline climbs trees with its agility and ease. As its arboreal acumen would imply, the margay dines mainly on birds obtained from passing limbs and branches. Small- to medium-sized mammals and a few select, easily-grabbed reptiles are also hunted. They are principally diurnal in habit and live almost exclusively in forests.

n.b.   *Margays have been kept as household pets, as have ocelots. The species's scarcity, however, has discouraged such irresponsible human proclivities.*

237

Mountain Cat

Felis jacobita

Portrait   To the average viewer, the mountain cat appears like any other unfamiliar wild cat, but taxonomists once considered this felid unique enough to merit a genus to call its own. The existence of its double-chambered bullae (the bony prominence behind the ear canal) earned the mountain cat the genus distinction *Oreailurus jacobita*. Today it has been relegated to "just" *Felis jacobita*. The body length is 23 inches (60 cm), with a tail that extends 14 inches (35 cm). The coloration is a pale silverish gray, marked by brown or orange-yellow markings; darker markings on the underbelly and limbs. The head is relatively large. The coat is fine and notably soft.

Distribution   Northeastern Chile, southern Peru, southern Bolivia and northern Argentina are the home of the Andes mountains where this wild cat roams.

Behavior   Dwelling at very high altitudes of the Andes, this species has acquired the common name Andean highland cat. Chinchillas and vizcachas, small burrowing mountain rodents, are pursued by this arid/semi-arid zone hunter.

n.b.   *The species is rarely observed but its aversion to snowfall has been repeatedly documented.*

Felis lynx

Northern Lynx

Portrait   Powerful legs, thick bones, and a full, heavy coat set apart the northern lynx as a hardy, widely distributed wild felid. The species stands 27 inches (68 cm) at the shoulder; body length can exceed 41 inches (105 cm). In color the lynx is yellowish brown covered by varying patches of darker browns, definition indefinite. In some subspecies, particularly on the North American continent, the spots are practically indiscernible. The fur is quite long and soft. The tail is black tipped.

Distribution   *Felis lynx* are indigenous to every continent except Antarctica and Australia. In North America, the lynx is found over Alaska, Canada and the northern United States; in Europe, though common in some areas, it is restricted compared to its once wide-spread forest distribution.

Behavior   Rarely roaming beyond its usual range, the lynx hunts by night by sight and scent; it can cover as much as 24 miles (40 km) in one night. These are terribly talented swimmers and climbers and ferocious fighters, utilizing their claws and teeth savagely. The snow hare is perhaps preferred for sustenance although lynxes hunt roe deer, red-legged partridges, mice and murine rodents, water voles, marmots, chamois, various game birds, as well as young boars and red deer. These are undoubtedly survivors that will prey on other wild cats, foxes, and dogs as the need dictates. Life span is 10–20 years.

n.b.   *Greek mythology personifies the lynx with the argonant Lynceus and bestows upon the pouncing and preponderant felid the ability to see through stone walls.*

Ocelot

Felis pardalis

John R. Quinn '90

Portrait   With prominent eyes and preeminent spots, the ocelot varies quite a lot in appearance from specimen to specimen. The softer ground color is covered by chainlike spots, each link individually outlined in black. The skull is fairly broad between the ears, which are small; the head is leopardlike in shape and striped. Body length varies but averages 39 inches (100 cm), the tail averages about 16 inches (40 cm). The height at the shoulders is 18 inches (45 cm) and the weight is about 29 pounds (14 kg).

Distribution   Less plenteous today in the United States than in the past, the ocelot is to be found in Arizona and southwestern Texas; its range extends south to Paraguay, northern Argentina, Colombia, Ecuador and northern Peru.

Behavior   The ocelot is an enduring species of feline that can be found in a variety of climes and habitats. In Brazil it hunts in the densest of forests, marshes and mountain forests as well; in Central America the ocelot thrives in the jungle heat. During the day, the cat sleeps in trees and is active at night, generally. It can hunt on the ground or in trees; actually leaping from tree to tree, the ocelot is able to usurp both monkey and bird. It is a competent swimmer and quite independent of its mate. Of all wild cats, the ocelot, unfortunately, suffers from having the greatest appeal as a home-kept pet. Thankfully, interest in keeping ocelots has waned—after injuring the species's numbers and individual animals, as well as their foolhardy keepers.

n.b.   *Ocelots communicate with their community through mewing and by always defecating in a specific place.*

Felis manul

Pallas Cat

Portrait   In appearance the pallas cat is quite similar to a medium-long-coated domestic cat. It is in fact only slightly bigger, weighing in at 7 or 8 pounds (2.5–3.5 kg). In length, the Pallas is 22 inches (57 cm) and the tail is about 10 inches (25 cm) long. The head is broad and short; the legs are short and stout; the ears are rounded bluntly, set low and wide at the base. The pallas's pelage is denser and longer than that of other wild felids. Its coloration is yellowish brown with darker agouti ticking; the hairs of the adult are white tipped and provide a silvery appearance. The tail is well furred and darkly ringed.

Distribution   Central Asia. The range moves along the eastern shore of the Caspian Sea through Turkmenistan, Uzbekistan, Kazakhstan, and Tibet, to Altai, Tuva, Mongolia, Iran and Afghanistan.

Behavior   Principally nocturnal in its hunting habits, the pallas cat or manul sleeps in burrows during the day. The manul depends on its sight to find its prey which consists almost exclusively of mouse hares and pikas. This cat hunts in fairly open country, as the low position of its ears facilitates minimal revealing of its head over a rock or brush. The pallas cat's eyes have been likened to the straight stare of the owl, and the cat is said to scream much like that horned predator to page a mate. When annoyed, the pallas does not hiss but rather produces a shrill through its closed teeth.

n.b.   *It has often been erroneously asserted that the pallas cat or steppe cat of central Asia was a direct ancestor of today's Persian breed. The variation in skulls provides no evidence towards such a lineage.*

Pampas Cat

Felis colocolo

Portrait The stoutly built pampas resembles the European wild cat in size, with less tail and a smaller head. Pointed ears and a wide face characterize this species and differentiate it from other South American wild cats. The pampas's pelage is plush and long, forming a mane about the neck; the tail is heavily plumed. Some specimens, however, can be nearly shorthaired. In color the pampas revels in earthtones which vary through yellows, grays, and browns. Bands of darker colors pattern the back; bars accentuate the eyes across the cheeks. Coloration varies between examples found in Chile and Argentina. At the shoulder, the pampas is 13 inches (33 cm) high; in length 27.5 inches (70 cm), plus 13 inches for the tail.

Distribution South America. Mountainous areas of Ecuador as well as grassy areas of Bolivia, Chile, Argentina, Peru, and Paraguay.

Behavior The *gato pejero* or grass cat is so-called because of its frequent habitation of grasslands; it has acquired that name in Argentina and extracts guinea pigs from those grasses. Pampas climb trees less often than many other wild cats and will do so only when being pursued. They otherwise remain terrestrial and hunt small land mammals (including burrowing birds). Although the pampas looks rather like a domestic cat, its disposition is far from domesticated and it is naturally aggressive.

n.b.   *The pampas has a particular liking of domesticated fowl.*

Puma

Felis concolor

John R. Quinn '90

Portrait One of the most handsome of all cats (and animals), the puma or cougar, as it is also known, has a nearly bullet-shaped head, relatively small, which rounds at the face. The ears are also rounded and small. The back legs are higher than the fore, and all fours are well muscled. The body appears lengthy and measures 63 inches (160 cm). The tail is cylindrical and well furred, measuring 33 inches (85 cm) in length. The male animal weighs about 185 pounds (82 kg), with females weighing substantially less. The pelage varies, depending on climate: it can be hard and bristly but soft, or long and soft. In color, the puma ranges the shades of brown; the muzzle and tail tip black; the underbody and facial points white.

Distribution America: North, Central and South. In North America, the species is numerous in the Rocky Mountain states, Texas and New Mexico, as well as California, Oregon and Washington in the coastal ranges; parts of Canada including Alberta and British Columbia.

Behavior The puma or mountain lion possesses the ability to adapt to a number of terrains, and at one point in the history of North America it was able to utilize that ability. Whether in the jungle, the prairie, the mountains or the tropics, the puma has been able to survive. While the animal rarely attacks man, it is a cruel and unstoppable hunter who has preyed upon deer, porcupine, wild horses, and sheep. Other various and sundry items have been recorded in studies of stomachs and droppings. Pumas are superior climbers and renowned wanderers.

Rusty-spotted Cat

Felis rubiginosa

John R. Quinn '89

Portrait   Smaller than our house-dwelling fur persons, the rusty-spotted cat is named for its large dark spots which mark the belly and limbs. The ground color is grayish and striped in brown or black. The face is also striped in white from the inner eye to the crest of the skull. The coat is fine and short. The tail is darker in color than the body. Body length averages 17 inches (42 cm) and the tail is 9 inches (24 cm) in length.

Distribution   Southern India and southern Ceylon are the only regions where the rusty-spotted cat has been positively identified.

Behavior   This cat is generally not considered a jungle dweller, although a Sri Lankan subspecies is known to enter the jungle. Rather the rusty-spotted cat prefers the open grass and brush, even drains in cleared area. The species in Ceylon is known to inhabit the forest and mountainous regions. It is typically nocturnal in its habits and preys on small mammals and birds. While the species has rarely been subjected to captivity, it has proven to be more tamable than many other wild cats. It is a greatly active feline that doesn't brag about its middling tree-climbing ability.

n.b.   *Its close relationship with the leopard cat (*Felis bengalensis) *once constituted their sharing the genus* Prionailurus; *today both species are among the genus* Felis.

Felis margarita

Sand Cat

Portrait   Well-developed cheeks flourished and furnished by well-developed whiskers, the sand cat has a broad face and big ears that give it a distinctive appearance. The coat, which is soft and dense, is sand-colored or straw-colored, varying from pale yellow to a darkish gray. The tail, which can be over 13 inches (34 cm) in length, is striped with dark brown rings. The feet are well padded and feathered for protection from the desert sands. Height at the shoulders is 10 inches (25 cm), and the body averages 20 inches (50 cm) in its length.

Distribution   Africa and western Asia. On the African continent, the species occurs in the northern Sahara, Senegal, Saudi Arabia and possibly Egypt; on the Asian continent, in the Kara Kum, Kizil Kum and Patta Kum deserts.

Behavior   Active during the twilight and/or dawn, this crepuscular sand dune pussy preys on various desert-dwelling rodents, including sand voles and jerboas; additionally it will make do with other small critters: reptiles, birds, hares and even locusts. Much if not all of the animal's water requirement is fulfilled through the body juices of its prey, since water is not available in the arid regions in which it lives. The paws are heavily padded to provide protection from the burning sands; the sand cat must be able to move across the desert without injuring its feet. Among the sand cat's natural enemies are the wolf, large birds of prey and snakes.

n.b.   *Much if not all of the animal's water requirement is fulfilled through the body juices of its prey, since water is not available in the arid regions in which it lives.*

Serval

Felis serval

John R. Quinn '90

Portrait   The graceful serval is characterized by its long legs and large oval ears. Its build is light and its tail quite short. The coat can be reddish yellow or just yellowish; it is marked with black spots which form stripes, lengthwise, on the animal's back. The legs, though long, are powerful and able to move the animal about with superior speed. Height: 21 inches (57 cm). Length of body: 32 inches (72 cm). Length of tail: 16 inches (40 cm). Average weight: 35 pounds (15 kg). The serval was once divided in two categories, the smaller type serval was called the servaline. This distinction is no longer applicable since the types have mixed and dissolved.

Distribution   Africa: throughout the sub-Sahara; variously and extensively across the continent; frequent occurrences in the western and central African tropical regions.

Behavior   This agile, nearly elastic, feline is active during the day and night; it is actually less nocturnal than other small African wild cats. The serval's carte du jour is varied: it is known to prey on grass rats, vlei rats, cane rats, hares, lizards and birds; it also is capable of downing smallish antelope. These are resourceful forest and grassland dwellers that have a natural affinity for water—they are superb swimmers! Their ears are key to their survival, keen enough to pinpoint the whereabouts of a burrowing rodent and mobile enough to flatten the head in sparse cover.

n.b.   *Popular zoo exhibits, these cats have been prey to hunters and their dogs; some tribes in Africa regard the serval's flesh as a delicacy.*

Snow Leopard

Panthera uncia

Portrait   Though often confused with the leopard, the snow leopard or ounce is smaller than the leopard, with a relatively elongated body and extensive tail. A short muzzle, vertical chin and high forehead detail the species's head study. The pelage is woolly—lengthy and thick. The legs are strong and of medium size. In color the snow leopard is a medium-dark gray, tinged by yellow on the flanks and white on the belly. The tail is well furred and well marked, with dark rings along its length. Height: 23 inches (60 cm). Body length averages 41–44 inches (104–112 cm); the tail is 35 inches (90 cm) in length.

Distribution   Along the southern slopes of the Himalayan range. From the Hindu Kush Mountains, Chitral, Gilgit, Hunza and the Karakoram Range eastward. Kashmir and Tibet.

Behavior   This is a large cat which appears more humble than other wild cats of its approximate size. The snow leopard, nevertheless, is a powerful, athletic cat who preys on wild animals in its path: wild goats, musk deer, wild boar and a variety of large game birds. It also stumbles upon the paths of some domestic animals, including sheep, goats, dogs, cows, yaks and horses (these latter few with less frequency, of course). It overtakes its prey by strangulation with its powerful jaws. Many snow leopards habitually find low-situated black vulture nests, and rest upon them.

n.b.   *The species is protected in some areas and its numbers continually expand; as bans increase, the demand for its fur diminishes.*

Spanish Lynx

Felis pardina

Portrait Powerful legs, thick bones, and a full, heavy coat set apart the Spanish lynx as a hardy, widely distributed wild felid. The species stands 27 inches (68 cm) at the shoulder; body length can exceed 41 inches (105 cm). The ears are prominent and tufted by long fur. Its paws are very large and tremendously furred in the winter, veritable snowshoes. In color the lynx is yellowish brown covered by varying patches of darker browns. In some specimens, the spots are practically indiscernible. The fur is quite long and soft. The tail is black tipped.

Distribution Restricted areas of Spain. In this country, the species is protected by the national park system.

Behavior The resilient and enduring Spanish lynx makes do in open forest areas or swamps. Rarely roaming beyond its usual range, the lynx hunts by night by sight and scent; it can cover as much as 24 miles (40 km) in one night. These are terribly talented swimmers and climbers and ferocious fighters, utilizing their claws and teeth savagely. For sustenance lynxes hunt roe deer, red-legged partridges and other game birds, mice and murine rodents, water voles, marmots, chamois, as well as young boars and red deer. These are undoubtedly survivors that will prey on other wild cats, foxes, and dogs as the need dictates.

n.b. *Despite man's delayed efforts of late, the species remains exceedingly rare.*

Felis temmincki # Temminck's Golden Cat

Portrait The body extends a length of 41 inches (104 cm) and is efficiently constructed. The tail does not taper but remains even across its over 15-inch (39-cm) length. The head is relatively large with short, round ears. In color, the ears are black, which contrast dramatically from the golden coloration of the pelt. The coat can vary from a yellow-brown to dark brown to red and gray. Melanistic or black specimens also occur and are particularly attractive. Spot and stripe patterns vary from locale to locale.

Distribution Southeastern Asia: Nepal, Sikkim, Assam, Burma, Tibet, China, Indochina, Siam, Malaya, and Sumatra.

Behavior Though separated by land spans of over 4000 miles (6400 km), Temminck's cat or Asiatic golden cat is a near relation of the African golden cat. There is much historical speculation concerning the development of these felids as two different species. C. Jacob Temminck, prominent Dutch naturalist, first described the species, and today the cat bears his name. Temminck's cat is an inhabitant of the woodlands and forest and has acquired a great many names from the Asians. It has been referred to as the yellow leopard, _huang poo,_ by Chinamen, and as the ''fire tiger'' by the Burmese. The cat is modestly particular about the components of its diet and will prey upon various birds or ground dwellers (as large as a water buffalo calf). It principally restricts itself to a terrestrial existence since it does not take well to climbing trees. Temminck's cats have responded fairly well in captivity.

_n.b._ _Kinky by human standards, Temminck's cat reserves its mating sessions to hollow trees, reports one Mishmi tribe near Tibet._

Tiger

Panthera tigris

John R. Quinn '90

Portrait The robust, massive body of the tiger cuts an undeniably imposing figure; the image of the striped tiger is nearly as vivid to imagine as that of the lion. The ground color varies but is essentially a shade of red (oranges to ochre); however, nearly white specimens are known to occur. The stripes, which bar the entire body, are gray, brown or black and their pattern is not standardized. The coloration on the muzzle, throat, whiskers, chest and underbody is white or cream. The length and thickness of the coat depend on the climate. The limbs are powerful; the body is long and the tail is typically half the body length, which can be guestimated at 110 inches (280 cm), accounting for the various subspecies. The Siberian, the largest variety, can weigh as much as 500 pounds (225 kg); the range for tigers is 220–500 pounds (100–225 kg).

Distribution Asia from Sumatra to Borneo north to Siberia. The largest existing populations appear to be in Nepal and India, and conceivably Bangladesh and Malaya.

Behavior The nocturnal tiger emerges from the restful dark forest to exercise omnipotent opportunism. This cat feeds on whatever is available and whatever it desires: boar, ox, deer, peacock, and fish. The puny piscines are assuredly a last resort if the land doesn't present an appetizing cast; reptiles even make the billing, not just tortoises, crocodiles too! These animals take to water with little reservation. Small bands of tigers often migrate together, as their reputation as wanderers precedes them.

250

Tiger Cat

Felis tigrina

Portrait   An attractive spot pattern adorns the ochre-shaded pelt of the tiger cat, also known as the little spotted cat. This pattern is enhanced by its gradually fading to the lighter color on the underbody, which nears white and lacks spots. The tail is ringed nearly a dozen times along its 13 inch (38 cm) length. Size in general varies notably but it is usually cited as about 21 inches (53 cm). This tiny feline weighs between 4–6 pounds (1.5–3 kg). The head is small and the ears are round tipped and fairly prominent. Twenty percent of the members of this species are melanistic.

Distribution   Central and South America: from Costa Rica to western Venezuela, Colombia, Ecuador, and likely northern Peru; through eastern Venezuela, Guiana and Brazil to Paraguay and Argentina (northern).

Behavior   The tiger cat, commonly referred to as the oncilla (translating to little leopard or jaguarette), is a forest dweller that has done well to hide its habits from inquiring human minds. This *poquito gato* has been bred in captivity; the gestation period lasts 75 days; one or two kittens per litter. These are professional hunters, and kittens develop their skills within the first two months of their lives. The male is considerably aggressive toward the female. Birds and small rodents probably comprise the oncilla's prey.

n.b.   *Experiments in captivity have yielded that the tiger cat has been "successfully" mated to a domestic cat, although about half the progeny was stillborn—an experiment not advisable to try at home.*

251

Bridled and Groomed—
the Domestics

Felis catus, *the domestic cat. American Shorthairs, silver chinchilla.*

Abyssinian

Portrait
HEAD: Never rounded or sharp, a moderate triangular shape graced by gentle contours. The muzzle marked by a shallow indentation is neither sharply pointed nor square. Rather large in proportion, the ears are well cupped, alert, moderately pointed—tipped and tufted. Bright, large eyes set wide apart, in an unstintingly unsquinting manner; possibly gazing to the East in Britain. Pencil markings under the eyes are characteristic.

BODY: Medium long, lithe with pleasing musculation. Legs, longer in the front than in the back, are slim and finely boned. Feet, small, oval, and compact—lightfooted. Tail is thick, long and tapering.

COAT: Short, fine textured; medium in length and resilient to touch and considerably thick. Double.

COLOR: Ruddy, red and blue coat colors are double or triple ticking with distinct, even, and contrasting dark- and light-colored bands. Ruddy brown is ticked with various shades of black or dark brown; it is sometimes called burnt sienna. Red coats are ticked with chocolate brown, with a deep red undercoat; color is warm throughout. Blue coats are a soft blue-gray, with slate blue ticking in various degrees; undercoat is ivory. Fawn, accepted by some associations, is a warm pinkish-buff ticked with a darker shade of pinkish-buff; undercoat is a pale oatmeal color. In all four colors, the undercoat is clear and bright to the skin. Eyes are gold or green, preference to rich, deep colors. Tail tips are colored darker according to darkest ticking.

Below: Abyssinian, red, owned by Tord and Suzanne Svenson. *Opposite:* Headstudy of the Svensons' red Aby, winner of Best Cat at the TICA Garden Show in 1988.

Origin   Resembling the African wild cat (*Felis libyca*), today's Abyssinian breed results from the selective breeding practices of early British fanciers. While the breed is ancient and pure compared to many others, it is unlikely that the Aby represents a direct, uninterrupted line to the entombed cats of Egypt. "Zula" was one of many feline souvenirs usurped from Abyssinia by British officers serving in northern Africa during the turmoil-filled period of the 1860s. The breed was first recognized in England in 1882 and was called the British Ticked. 1919 marks the formation of the Abyssinian Cat Club and the adoption of the Abyssinian name. Addis Ababa, born in 1935, was the first American-born Abyssinian.

Personality   Perceptive and intelligent, the well-schooled Aby is alert and discriminating. Socialization is tantamount to the extroverted vaudevilling feline: dignified jesters and soothing minstrels, these are cats of sublime affections and talent.

Abyssinians, red and ruddy, owned by the Gilmans.

Ruddy adult and kittens owned by Richard and Leslie Gilman.

Preferred Person An attentive and outgoing human able to provide spicy outlets and diversions to engross the Aby's active mind and body.

Grooming Once-over brushing to remove loose hairs and regular nail clipping comprise the easycare grooming of this sleekly coated breed.

Breeding Generally considered difficult due to less fecund females, large kitten skulls, and small litter sizes. At most, two to three kittens to be expected per litter, with one per litter common. Aby queens are reportedly more susceptible to miscarriage and injury than are those of many other breeds.

Palatables Never vegetarian, many Abys prefer beef to poultry and fish, though never refuse an occasional duck or lobster, if seasonable.

Proclivities & Prejudices Favor picture windows, leather hassocks, and open gardens (preferably hanging); fancy the flight of the sacred ibis or any other passing, notably extinct avian wonder.

American Bobtail

Portrait

HEAD: Broad with strong jaws. The ears, medium-large in size, are wide at the base and set well down. The nose is nearly straight with a gentle break permitted. The eyes are large and slightly rounded in shape.

BODY: Slightly longer than tall, stocky, appearing quite low to the ground. Distinctive differences in males and females: males should be heavily built, muscular and wide-shouldered; females similarly built but with a marked feminine suggestion. The legs are short and heavily boned. Tail must be present with a preferred length of 1–4 inches; often flexible and knotted, ending in a knot or point.

COAT: Medium-length coat, plush and non-matting; length ranges from medium-short to medium-long. The latter length may reveal neck furnishings and pants.

COLOR: All colors and patterns are acceptable; eyes of the colorpoint are blue, while all others possess eyes that correspond to coat color.

Origin Serendipity in the sixties: a cross between a well-acquainted feline pair, a seal point Siamese female and a short-tailed tabby male of unknown parentage. Their offspring were delightful, and interested parties incorporated Birman, Himalayan, and Himalyan/Siamese-cross cat into the pool. Success bobbed up and down until more qualified breeders worked to revive and stabilize the cat which was the American Bobtail. While the numbers in the United States are small today, dedicated breeders are enthusiastic about this experimental's gaining acceptance.

Personality In temperament the Bobtail is super; in personality the breed cannot be described in one word—bright, lively, sweet, intelligent and loving—incomparable and fabulous. These are devoted and elegant felines capable of charming the tail off any cat lover.

Preferred Person Partial to Americans, perhaps, the American Bobtail craves human attention. Flattering and perceptive human most desirable.

Grooming The non-matting coat requires once-overs with a large fine-toothed comb. Avoid oil-based shampoos since they will alter the coat texture, leaving it silky and flat.

Breeding Balanced head-to-toe, the American Bobtail has no breeding oddities. Rumpies (tailless cats), full-length tails and dock tails are all unacceptable. The ideal tail is 1–4 inches.

Palatables People food is fun, but not always good for the growing (or even adult) kitty.

Proclivities & Prejudices Not impartial to canines, whose housewarming and greeting rituals they imitate. Swinging doors are frowned upon.

American Bobtail, white with brown, owned by Kim Wiegman.

American Curl

Portrait

HEAD: A modified wedge shape; it is medium, more long than wide. The muzzle is neither pointed nor square, with gentle contours. Muzzle break should be free of pinch or snippiness. The chin is firm. The Curl's ears are paramount to the breed's uniqueness: they are wide at the base with rounded tips that curve back in a smooth arc. This curl should be attractive and obvious. The ears are erect with interior furnishings extending. The eyes are walnut shaped and moderately large.

BODY: Semi-foreign, not cobby. A medium-size cat whose length is one and one-half-times the shoulder height. Weight: 5–10 pounds (2.5 to 4.5 kg). The musculation is moderately developed and well toned. The tail is wide at the base and tapering, proportionately long. The legs are medium with like boning. Paws, round and medium.

COAT: Medium long, flat lying; not bushy; silky in texture. Tail is well plumed. The longer variant has a minimal undercoat. No ruff.

COLOR: Any and all colors, as the breed is descended from domestic short-hairs; the foundation cat was black.

Below: American Curl, blue and white bicolor, owned by Caroline Scott. *Opposite:* American Curl, black and white bicolor, owned by Geri Hamilton.

Origin Serendipity and spontaneity set up the story of the American Curl: serendipitously, Joe and Grace Ruga discovered "Shulamith" outside their Lakewood, California, home; this longhaired black stray proved to be more than just another Southern California mutant—she was a spontaneous mutant! Genetically speaking, that is, even though Shulamith *was* quick-thinking and acted on impulse. The mutation of course was in her wonderful, wondrous ears, curled forward gracefully. This "black but comely" kitty (as her name translates) would become the foundation for the new breed. Through the course of a few years and the right cat-world contacts, these unique cats were recognized by two major American registries.
Personality Patient and curious, Curls are favored for their excellent mousing and child-rearing instincts. They are gregarious with adults and other cats too; intelligence is astonishing, as is charm.

American Curl, solid black (the color of "Shulamith"), owned by Anne Wilson.

American Curl with tabby markings akin to the American Shorthair, including the forehead "M."

Preferred Person Open-minded, inquisitive human with positive outlook on life and a sincere unfabricated loathing for mice.

Grooming The silky, lustrous coat of both the short and long coats requires consistent grooming.

Breeding The ear angle mutation is a simple dominant and therefore requires that only one parent possess it. Outcrosses are being attempted by breeders; no adverse abnormalities are known. Kittens mature in two to three years.

Palatables Pressed lunch meat and spicy bologna, other pseudo-meats too, fresh meat and canned cat food are equally enjoyed.

Proclivities & Prejudices Donkey rides, rose gardens, well-tanned beefy surfers, sixties' rock, and soft-spoken hairdressers.

American Shorthair

Portrait

HEAD: Oblong (slightly longer than wide), with unquestionably full cheeks. Muzzle squared. Ears erect, slightly rounded tips, medium in size. Eyes round, wide, with upper rim giving an almond shape.

BODY: Medium to large, typically larger than the British Shorthair. Heavy shoulders and well-developed chest comprise a solid build, with no exaggeration; symmetry strongly considered. Wellmuscled and firmly boned, the legs are medium in length. Paws are full, firm and rounded; pads heavy. Tail, medium long, heavy at base.

COAT: Though short, the coat is thick and well suited to colder temperatures. Even and hard in texture.

COLOR: Besides a deep rich red, a pure glistening white, and a sound light blue, the breed displays coats of black, cream, chinchillas, smokes, tabbies, patches, and bi-colors. Except chocolate and lilac, the American Shorthair unfurls every possible color, quite similar to the Persian (Longhair). Tabby patterns, for which the breed is especially renowned, can be divided into three patterns. The classic tabby pattern is marked by broad, clearly defined dense markings. Legs are barred evenly with bracelets which stack high to meet the body. Tail is evenly ringed. The letter "M" is formed on the forehead by frown marks. The shoulder markings flirt a unique butterfly pattern. In the mackerel tabby pattern, contrasting light and dark bands comprise the ground color. Dark necklaces; narrow leg bracelets; an unbroken dark band down the back; the tail is affluently ringed. The patched tabby is an established brown, silver or blue tabby with patches of red and/or cream. According to coat color, eyes can be brilliant gold, copper, green or blue-green, and hazel.

Below: American Shorthair, cameo silver tabby, owned by Hedy Casperson. ***Opposite:*** Headstudy of American Shorthair, classic red tabby, owned by Claire Harden.

American Shorthair, classic red tabby, owned by Claire Harden, feigning a most utilitarian image.

Origin   Utilitarian in stock, the American Shorthair traces to the cargo bins of the Mayflower. Like the pilgrims themselves, these no-nonsense cats staked their claims and hard-earned their daily bread on the strange new land. Hardly Puritan, however, in proliferation, the cats bred uninhibitedly and liberally with any and all consenting strays. Surveying the barns of agrarians and cabins of frontiersmen, the American Shorthair, once called the Domestic Shorthair, endured and thrived. Although the first registered Shorthairs in America were of British origin, "Buster Brown" in 1904 was the first home-bred cat to lace up registration, unashamedly revealing his alley cat ancestry.

Personality   A true terrier of a cat, consistent and pragmatic in its execution of its daily routine and furry finds. A mouser of skill and enthusiasm; acrobatic and aerobic when awake, content when napping. Responds generously to most every human member of the family and does well with canines and other felines alike.

Preferred Person Any human simple enough to whistle "Yankee Doodle" loud, and smart enough not to bother his cat with it.

Grooming A healthy brushing of the coat is worthwhile; acclimate the kitten to this early so that the adult doesn't protest dramatically.

Breeding Fundamental and without unusual considerations; typical litter size is four.

Palatables Commercial cat food generally preferred, supplemented by a treat or an ill-fated bite-size rodent.

Proclivities & Prejudices Soft country music and absolute stillness. American Shorthairs insist that everything in their presence remain still or be prepared to be pounced upon; senior cats tend to ignore objects that go bump or boo, by night or by day.

American Shorthair, silver classic tabby. Note the heavily ringed tail and dark necklaces.

American Wirehair

Portrait

HEAD: Well proportioned, round, with prominent cheeks. This roundness of skull is different from the oblong quality called for in the American Shorthair. Muzzle is well developed. Chin is firm and well developed. Slightly rounded at the tips, the ears are medium in size and set wide apart. Eyes are large, round, also set well apart.

BODY: Medium to large. Torso proportionate and well rounded, appearing cobby and muscular. Legs are medium boned and of moderate length, well muscled. The paws are oval and compact; pads substantial. Tail is neither blunt nor pointed, tapering from the rounded rump.

COAT: Wire, of course, and coarse, as well as crimped, resilient, hooked, springy, and curly. This wiry fur is medium length and dense, giving the breed its most unique outer covering and name.

COLOR: Solid colors including white, black, blue, red, and cream; chinchillas in silvers and reds; smokes in black, blue, and red; tabbies in silver, red, brown, blue, and cream, never patched; also tortoiseshell, calicos, and bicolors. Eye colors usually brilliant gold, but may be green, blue-green or hazel, according to coat color. Hybridizations will result in other colors, including chocolate, lavender, the Himalayan pattern, or these in combination with white; eye color surely will vary. In solid white-colored cats, odd eyes must be blue and gold.

Below: American Wirehair, red and white bicolor, owned by Richard H. Gebhardt. *Opposite:* Headstudy of American Wirehair, tortoiseshell and white, owned by Gebhardt.

Origin While numerous and less accountable mutants have emerged in the State of New York, not all have proven to breed true. The forecat of the American Wirehair breed was such a mutant felid. In Verona, New York, Council Rock Farmhouse Adam of Hi-Fi was kittened in 1966. His coat was coarse and hooked, though quite sparse, and notably different from his Shorthair siblings. Inbreeding to Adam's sister produced progeny with fuller and more woolly coats, still coarse of course. The new "breed" took hold rather quickly throughout North America and was first exhibited in 1978. Although the breed is not the most handsome of companion felines, they are indeed different and have "hooked" many American fanciers, although Britain remains largely disinterested.

Headstudy of American Wirehair owned by Richard H. Gebhardt.

American Wirehair owned by Gebhardt.

Personality Committed and energetic, the American Wirehair is a free thinker and a free-lance hunter. Maintaining the same love of play and sport as its American Shorthair cousin, the Wirehair cavorts without hesitation. Sincere and affectionate.

Preferred Person A straightforward, easily assimilated individual with an eye for the unique; rural inhabitant in need of silo lookout.

Grooming Not extensive; curls should not become wavy from a brush-happy human. Coat is resistant and nearly self-maintaining.

Breeding The wire gene (*Wh*) is transmitted as a normal autosomal dominant, meaning that no lethal or hazardous potential exists; breeding is usual, in a usual way; four kittens the average. Outcrosses to the American Shorthair are permissible.

Palatables Homecooked meals, natural ingredients; not an irregular quantity of fiber.

Proclivities & Prejudices May shun a household of neurotic or high-strung humans, though does enjoy an occasional sideshow-type diversion. Tree climbing is enjoyed half the time. Open views, minds and spaces.

Balinese

Portrait

HEAD: Long, tapering wedge which is of medium size and always in absolute proportion to the body. Beginning at the nose, the wedge proceeds in straight lines to the ear tips, without breaking at the whiskers. Muzzle is fine and wedge shaped. Ears are strikingly large, and wide at base. Almond-shaped eyes are medium in size and slant towards the nose in an appealing Oriental fashion.

BODY: Medium size; well muscled, lithe, and slender. Legs are long and slim, in fine proportion to the body. Paws are dainty, small and oval. Tail is quite long, thin, and tapering to a point; the tail hair resembles a plume.

COAT: A long, silky single coat; without a mane, atypical of other long-haired breeds. Ears are well feathered.

COLOR: As with the Siamese, there are four possible colorpoints, which include: seal point, chocolate point, blue point, and lilac point. In the seal point the body is an even pale fawn to cream, becoming lighter on the belly and chest; points are a deep seal brown; tone is always warm. In the chocolate point the body is ivory, without shading; points are milk chocolate in color; tone is warm. In the blue point the body is bluish white, frosting to white on stomach and chest; tone, of course, is cold. In the lilac point a snowy white is highlighted with frosty gray points; tone connotes a pink. Eye color for all four colorpoints is a deep vivid blue.

Below: Balinese, blue point, owned by Marjorie Bergen. Opposite: Balinese, seal point, owned by Bergen.

Origin The city of Singaraja, situated on the northern coast of Bali on the Bali Sea, has thrived in creating a culture and tradition all its own—unfortunately, the beautiful Balinese breed has never graced any such southeastern Asian island. The Balinese doesn't feign any romantic ancient origin other than its undeniable affiliation to the Siamese. Essentially the breed is a longhaired Siamese cat, and that name was employed in the 1950s when the mutation first occurred in the U.S. Siamese fanciers, however, objected to the use of "Siamese" and Longhair fanciers contrived the name "Balinese," if only for its ring and glamorous appeal. Some believe that the agile and balletlike movement of the new breed was similar to the native dancers of Bali, and that this influenced the name choice.

Personality Active and affectionate to the *n*th degree. Likes a specified amount of attention and will clarify the given moments with unmistakable politeness. While not an outdoor cat, the Balinese is as talented a gymnast and sportsman as any, and excels most in grace and balance.

Preferred Person A tidy, upbeat human who delights in eating to kettledrum music and reading James Michener, but necessarily one individual willing to concede to the Balinese's moods and whims.

Grooming The medium-long length of the Bali's coat makes it less likely to tangle and mat than the Persian, though regular brushing and combing are still essential, as they are to other longhaired breeds.

Balinese, lilac-lynx-point, owned by Nancy P. French.

Balinese, chocolate point, owned by Marjorie A. Bergen.

Breeding   Cats reach sexual maturity earlier than other longhaired breeds. Litter size is average and outcrosses to Siamese are allowable; such kittens will have medium feltlike coats.

Palatables   Despite the rumors from certain circles, Balinese are not partial to pineapple, except maybe for an occasional, unexpected tropical sortie (of sorts). Otherwise, not selective.

Proclivities & Prejudices   Open terraces, bird baths, kittens (and puppies sometimes); often disregards prime-time television.

Bengal

Portrait

HEAD: Broad modified wedge, with rounded contours. Longer than wide, it appears slightly small in proportion to body. Nose bridge extends above the eyes. Nose is large and wide. Muzzle full and broad, with large prominent whisker pads and high pronounced cheekbones. Eyes are large, set wide apart, and oval (may be slightly almond shaped). Ears are medium small, basically short, with wide base and rounded tips.

BODY: Long and substantial, its high degree of musculature is a distinguishing feature. Robustly boned, it is a large cat, though smaller than the largest of domestics. Legs are medium long, longer in back than front, very muscular, never delicate. Paws are round and large. Tail is thick, tapered at the end, with a rounded tip; medium-large in size, and medium in length.

COAT: Short to medium in length, possibly longer on kittens, it is thick, luxuriant, and distinctively soft to the touch.

COLOR: All variations of the brown spotted tabby are allowed, but yellow, buff, tan, golden and orange are preferred. Bengals exhibit three color groups: leopard, snow leopard, and marble leopard. Spots are random or occur horizontally; they may be black, brown, tan, or any of various shades of chocolate or cinnamon. Rosettes formed by a partial circle of spots around a distinctly red center are preferable to single spotting.

*Below: Bengal, leopard, owned by Michael E. Nelson. **Opposite:** Headstudy of Bengal, leopard, owned by Ruth Hodges.*

Above: Bengal, leopard, owned by Gene Johnson of Gogees Cattery. ***Opposite:*** Bengal, snow leopard, owned by Jean Mill.

Origin   In an attempt to preserve the aura of the Asian leopard cat, an exquisite species fighting extinction in the forest wilds of Asia, Jean Sugden crossed a member of the species with a domestic cat in 1963. Her breeding program then paused for about twenty years. With the assistance of Dr. Willard Centerwall, who had been working with the cat throughout the 1970s, Mrs. Jean Sugden Mill began again with fervor to capture the pattern, color, and characteristics of the leopard cat in a domestic/wild hybrid. (Egyptian Maus were the domestic typically used for outcrossing.) Through careful selection and strict breeding practices, Mrs. Mill, in conjunction with a handful of others, including Dr. Centerwall, Mrs. Ethel Hawser, and Dr. Gregg Kent, produced the sound base from which today's Bengal has burgeoned.

Personality   Docile and determined, the Bengal blooms in the modern home, bringing hints of the wild in its stalking, retrieving, and water play. Essentially encompassing the full spectrum of feline personality, the Bengal is independent when it wants but mostly outgoing and affectionate.

Preferred Person   The human with a true, deep appreciation of nature, one who watches quietly and listens with concentrated attention.

Grooming   The medium-length, characteristically soft coat wears best when groomed daily. Ideally the groomer employs smooth, effortless, nearly affectionate strokes with a natural-bristle brush.

Breeding   Males of first generation leopard crosses and most F_2 hybrid males are sterile. Qualified outcrosses are allowed; only F_1 and F_2 females should be outcrossed. Bengals should have at least one-sixteenth wild ancestry.

Palatables   Always civilized and most domestic, Bengals dine delightfully on duck l'orange and iced oysters.

Proclivities & Prejudices   Favor the scent of summer savory and saffron threads; play zestfully with spools and splash refreshingly in puddles.

Birman
Sacred Cat of Burma

Portrait

HEAD: Broad, round and strong. Cheeks are full; muzzle, rounded. Chin is strong and well developed. Rounded at the tip, the ears are medium in length; they are broad based and set well apart. Eyes are roundish in shape, with the outer corner tipping *ever* so slightly upward.

BODY: Long and well developed; the legs are thick set and medium in length; the paws are large, round, and firm. Tail is medium in length and proportioned well to the body.

COAT: Fur is longish and silky in texture. Neck is adorned with a profuse ruff; fur on belly is slightly curly. Coat never mats.

COLOR: Four colorpoints occur: seal point, blue point, chocolate point, and lilac point. In the seal point, the body is an even pale to cream, becoming lighter on the belly and chest; points are a deep seal brown, except the gloves which are pure white; tone is always warm. In the blue point, the body is bluish white to pale ivory, shading towards white on the stomach and chest; tone is cold. In the chocolate point, the body is ivory, with no shading; points are milk chocolate in color, except the gloves which are pure white; tone is warm. In the lilac point, a pearl or off-white is accentuated with gray points, except the gloves which are pure white; tone is pinkish. Eye color for all four Birman colors tends toward violet, which is to say a deepish blue.

Below: Birman, seal point, owned by Betty A. Cowles. *Opposite:* Birman, blue point, owned by Connie Webb.

Birman, blue point, researching its origin.

Origin Preserved in legend, the Birman's origins affiliate today's breed with the revered cats once kept in the Buddhist temples of Burma. The devout holymen and wet rice farmers of the Indo-Chinese nation long sanctified the pure white-pawed felines, who once communicated with the goddess of Death. The cats followed the priests to Tibet whence they were ushered to Europe by French and British military men who received them as gifts from the Burmese clerics. In France, the breed was aptly dubbed the Sacred Cat of Burma. French imports reached the U.S. in 1959, and Britain six years later. The Birman is not to be confused with the short-coated Burmese, who is not Burmese nor associated with Burma in any way. It is not known how pure today's Birman breed actually is, since the Siamese coloration and the Persian coat quality seem to suggest both breeds being used at some point.

Personality Mannerly and sensitive, though often buzzing with energy and play, rivetingly rambunctious. The singular elegance of the Birman's eyes and fascinating expression separate this breed as one of the most dignified of all cats, domestic or wild.

Preferred Person A human with monklike principles, not afraid to let his hair down or shave his head, as the occasion dictates.

Grooming Regular coat care is essential to keep the Birman's long fur in optimum condition.

Breeding Females are prolific and make attentive mothers. Outcrosses to the Siamese and Persian are never permitted. Birman kittens are light colored, acquiring darker points at 10–12 weeks.

Palatables Tend to be Oriental in tastes: white, boneless fish and rice agree with many Birman appetites; lo mein to chow. Others opt for meat dishes.

Proclivities & Prejudices Pantries and pedestals, ice cubes on marble floors, well-polished and dusted furniture; loves intolerable mothers-in-law.

Birman, seal point.

Bombay

Portrait

HEAD: Without flat planes the skull is attractively round and chubby cheeked. A short, strong muzzle with a visible break, never appearing pug or snub. Considerable breadth between the eyes and tapering. Chin should be firm and set well, indicating the proper bite. Eyes and ears set far apart. Ears, tilting forward, are broad at the base and medium in size, with tips slightly rounded. Eyes are round.

BODY: In development, muscular; in size, medium. Body must not appear rangy, although males tend to be significantly larger. The Bombay must be perfectly proportioned; legs in harmony with body and tail. Paws are round. Tail is straight, neither short nor whippy.

COAT: Like satin in texture, the coat is fine and short, very glossy, shining with an almost artificial sheen.

COLOR: Black. As in the Indian black leopard, black is uniform on the entire body, including the pads, with no shading to the hairs. Eye color ranges from gold to copper, always deep and bright.

*Below: Bombay, owned by Janet Becker. **Opposite:** Headstudy of Becker's Bombay. Body color is invariably black; eye color is always deep and bright, from gold through copper.*

Origin The Bombay is another example of Americans' experimenting with established breeds, being pleased with their accomplishments, and accrediting the name to totally *non sequitur* places. The Bombay is a hybrid emerging from crosses of the Burmese and the American Shorthair. Its jet black coat and aloof, self-contained expression liken it to the Indian melanistic leopard and thus Bombay (an Indian city) was selected as the new breed's name. The breed emerged in the early 1970s and was registered by major organizations in 1976. The breed's invariably black coat color, vivid copper eyes and sleek physical conformation set it apart from other cats and speak well for this purebred cat's individualistic qualities.

Personality Like the rather vociferous Burmese, the Bombay is outgoing and quite nosy. The breed's intelligence is clearly denoted in its expression and controlled in-house meandering. A truly charming animal to have in the home with little desire to roam, despite its American Shorthair cousin's blood. There are always exceptions, be assured.

Preferred Person Level-headed, predictable human not given to spontaneous gatherings or unruly human friends. A peace-loving homebody is Nirvana.

Grooming Minimal care required outside weekly or bi-weekly once-overs with a brush. Frequent petting is helpful too.

Breeding Litters range from four to five kittens. Outcrosses to black American Shorthairs and sable Burmese are allowable. Kittens should totally darken by six months of age.

Palatables Light lunches for adult cats; young kittens are always hungry. Appetites are moderate and preferences few.

Proclivities & Prejudices Loud music and boisterous children are unexceptionally detested and avoided. Enjoys the autumn months when poorly behaved children are most impressionable.

Opposite: Bombay owned by Marianne Flansburg.
Despite the solid black of the Bombay, the breed is
among the cat world's most colorful!

British Shorthair

Portrait

HEAD: Circular and massive, the head is marked by round bone structure; the forehead, too, should be rounded with a flattish plane on the top of the skull. The nose is broad and medium in size. The chin is firm and well developed. Equally developed is the muzzle, which is distinctive for this breed. A recognizable stop beyond the whisker pads. Medium-size ears are rounded at the tips and broad at the base, always set far apart, yet completely harmonious to the roundness of the skull. The eyes are alert and large, decidedly round.

BODY: Medium to large, the body is well put together and sturdy; the back is level, the chest broad and deep. The legs are powerful and medium-short in length. Paws round and firm. The tail, in sync with body balance, is medium length, thicker at base and tapering.

COAT: Short, resistant and resilient—well-bodied single coat, never woolly.

COLOR: The breed displays coats of red, white, blue, black, cream, chinchillas, smokes, tabbies, patches, and bi-colors. The British Shorthair occurs in every possible color, quite similar to the Persian (Longhair), including in the United Kingdom lilac, chocolate, red, blue classic tabby, chocolate tortoiseshell, lilac tortie, blue tortie and white, and shorthair colorpoint. Tabby patterns are divided into three patterns. The classic tabby pattern is marked by broad, clearly defined dense markings. Legs are barred evenly with bracelets which stack high to meet the body. Tail is evenly ringed. The letter "M" is formed on the forehead by frown marks. The shoulder markings unfurl a unique butterfly pattern. In the mackerel tabby pattern, contrasting light and dark bands comprise the ground color. Dark necklaces; narrow leg bracelets; an unbroken dark band down the back; the tail is well ringed. The patched tabby is an established brown, silver or blue tabby with patches of red and/or cream. According to coat color eyes can be brilliant gold, copper, green or blue-green, and hazel. Whites can occur in blue-eyed, orange-eyed, or odd-eyed varieties; odd eyes are sapphire blue and orange, copper or golden.

Opposite: British Shorthair, blue and white bicolor, owned by M.J. Egeri and M.J. Osborne. In Great Britain, the British Shorthair is divided into individual breeds by color; hence, the British Bicolor Shorthair. There are ten individual breeds in all.

Origin Images of rugged street-dwelling felines on the shoulders of Roman troops into England recreate the beginnings of the Shorthair in Britain. While these cats populated alleys, parks and pubs for generations, it wasn't until cat fancier Harrison Weir intervened that the British Shorthair (as a breed) became involved in the exhibition world taking hold in the late nineteenth century. For a time, the British Shorthair was the most popular cat in show ring circles. The imported, lushly coated Persian's arrival usurped the British Shorthair's place for a few decades prior to World War II. In Britain today, the Shorthair is divided by color and each is considered an individual breed. In the U.S. they remain clumped as one breed, as is the American Shorthair, the States suburban equivalent.

Personality Pliable and hardy, it is the average Briton's (as well as the above-average Briton's) image of cat-about-town. Sometimes reserved with tea-time quaintness, other times high-spirited and cocky, in a cockney sort of way. In short, very British.

British Shorthair, white, owned by Karri Scharff-Huemer.

British Shorthair, blue, waxing patriotic. Great Britain, home of the original Red Coat, takes pride in and credit for perfecting the feline blue coat.

Preferred Person Any chap with a colourful outlook on life; any human who understands and accepts the feline's natural right to the universe.

Grooming Self-cleaning, self-grooming, self-determined. Attempt to groom from kittenhood, or just throw in the towel. Bathing is expressly prohibited—"Wet me, you die!"

Breeding Despite physical similarities to American Shorthair, such an outcross is not allowed. Litter size is average: three or four.

Palatables Milk in its tea, crumpets without tedium, pudding required on holidays at least.

Proclivities & Prejudices Abhors being wet, even by the rain. Fog is often appreciated, if spectated through a window. Doesn't mind a canine who knows his place.

Burmese

Portrait

HEAD: Somewhat rounded, with outstanding breadth between ears. The wide cheek bones taper towards a blunt wedge. The chin is rounded and firm; proper bite is imperative. Medium in size, the ears are well set apart and tilt forward to insure alertness. The eyes are set far apart and rounded in appearance, with a straight Oriental slant towards the nose; the lower line remains rounded.

BODY: Medium in size, no matter on what side of the Atlantic the cat lives. American cats need to be compact while British cats should be of a foreign type with a longer appearance, not approaching the svelte, slender appearance of the Siamese, however.

COAT: Glossy, fine and satinlike, close-lying and resilient. The glossiness of the Burmese's coat is a celebrated feature of the breed.

COLOR: Burmese occur in a number of colors, regardless of which registry accepts what. Originally sable brown was *the* color for the breed; in the U.K. the color is described as seal brown and called simply brown. In the U.S. three other colors occur: champagne, described as a warm honey beige, shading toward a light goldish tan; blue, a medium tone with warm fawn undertones; and platinum, a silvery gray with pale fawn undertones. These three colors were once registered as a separate breed known as the Malayan. In England the following colors are recognized as well: red, brown tortie, cream, blue tortie, chocolate tortie, and lilac tortie.

*Below: Burmese, sable and champagne, owned by Herb Zwecker. **Opposite:** Burmese, sable, owned by Diane Quaas-Lopez. Sable is the traditional color of the Burmese breed.*

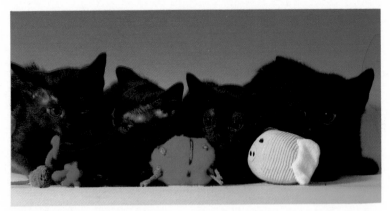

*Above: Burmese kittens owned by Diane Quaas-Lopez. **Opposite:** Burmese, sable.*

Origin   First recognized in 1936 and today recognized around the world, the Burmese is a product of many years of meticulous litter selection. Referred to as a "mutational breed" (for its original color would have been black or tabby), the Burmese traces to a brown Oriental-type female, named Wong Mau, who was mated to an excellent quality Siamese. Though the litter was rather unsightly, representing neither breed well but rather appearing as a poor mix, by re-crossing one of the litter to the Oriental type, the preferred brown color was improved. Dr. Joseph Thompson is credited as being of the first to attend to the breed, one of many foreign types indigenous to Asia.

Personality   Delighting its owner with vocal antics, the Burmese comes standard with a full range of sound. In intelligence, curiosity, and problem-solving ability, the breed is superb. For the owner who desires a cat with zest, a companion with character, and pet none too shy to get into trouble, the Burmese is ideal.

Preferred Person   Though unselective in its audience, the Burmese reportedly fares best with a concert-goer or any auditory-oriented, attentive other; it requires a human cognizant of the feline's antics, its message, and its need for reciprocation.

Grooming   Short coated, the breed generally requires little in the way of brushing or combing, though a firm rubdown with a dampened terrycloth or grooming glove is most appreciated and helpful in keeping the coat clean.

Breeding   Litter size typically borders on five, with individuals attaining sexual maturity at about seven months.

Palatables   Hardy and long-lived, the Burmese simply requires a balanced feline diet with no untypical need for the tongue of cow or toad.

Proclivities & Prejudices   In a home with a piano, the Burmese is certain to pass afternoons atop it, purring melodiously, anticipating accompaniment. Truly the diva.

California Spangled

Portrait

HEAD: Sculpted in shape, with wide cheekbones; medium in both length and width. The forehead is slightly domed; the muzzle, full; the chin and jaw, strong. In profile, the stop is gentle between the forehead and nose. The ears are rounded at tips and medium in size, with base and height equal. The eyes are open, almond shaped and medium-large in size.

BODY: Long, lean, medium in size, carried low and even like a hunter; overall musculature is well-developed. A solid frame well supported on strong and ample legs with particularly strong thighs. The feet are medium in size. The tail is blunt tipped, medium full throughout.

COAT: Short, velvety, and close lying on back, sides, neck and face; somewhat more lengthy on tail and underbelly, though still short.

COLOR: A patterned, unmistakably spotted cat; markings themselves are blocked or rounded in shape (triangular, round, square and oval are permissible). Colors include: silver, charcoal, bronze, gold, red, blue, brown and black. Tail tip on all colors is black. A dark bar marks the top of each foreleg. Eye colors are fixed for each coloration: amber to brown, cocoa to gray-brown, and sand.

Origin Poachers and furriers knowingly ensure the encroaching extinction of many wild cat species. A blueprint was drawn in the early 1970s for a breed of domestic cat which would pay tribute to the passing of so many spotted wild felids and concurrently celebrate that coat pattern, distracting people's needs to indulge in the furs of endangered species. Six common breeds were incorporated as well as a feral Egyptian cat and a tropical house cat from Southeast Asia. Considering the cost of the California Spangled, only those who would bundle themselves in expensive furs could afford to purchase such an exclusive West Coast feline starlet.

Personality Expressive and well-tempered, the California Spangled is sufficiently active, even athletic. Intelligent beyond the average feline.

Preferred Person A human who enjoys face-to-face human-feline contact, respects the feline personality and all of nature.

Grooming The velvety coat requires little grooming.

Breeding Kittens are all born totally black, except for white chin, spectacles, and interior white ear; they frost as they mature. "Snow leopard" is the term for the recessive phase; it is not a true color.

Proclivities & Prejudices Allergies to department stores; favors synthetic fabrics and new age music.

Above: Headstudy of California Spangled, snow leopard. *Below:* California Spangled, silver. Photos courtesy of California Spangled Cat Association, Paul Casey, president.

Chartreux

Portrait

HEAD: Broad and round, though not entirely spherical. The jaws are powerful, the cheeks full. The contour of the forehead is soft and high; the nose of medium size and straight; stop easily discernible at eye level. The muzzle is quite small, tapering and narrow. The eyes, expressive and appealing, are rounded; the ears, set rather high on the head, are medium in size and always erect.

BODY: Physique is athletic: robust and well developed; the shoulders are broad, the chest deep. Bone and muscle are solid and comparatively massive. Males are larger than females, although both sexes are good-size animals. The legs are of medium length, fine boned though sturdy. The paws are round and medium in size, tending towards the dainty side.

COAT: The coat is slightly woolly in texture ("should break like a sheepskin at neck and flanks," if that helps); in length it is medium-short. Older cats tend to exhibit a greater degree of wool; males more so.

COLOR: Various shades of blue-gray which vary from dark to light, ash to slate. The blue-gray coat is a hallmark of the Chartreux: all parts of the cat's body are grayish, except the eyes which are a golden copper and the paw pads which are rose-taupe. The lips are blue and the nose leather is slate gray.

*Below: Chartreux, owned by Debbie Rexelle. **Opposite:** Headstudy of Rexelle's Chartreux.*

Origin From Buffon, Linneaus, and Lesson, scholars have ascertained the probability of the Chartreux's drifting down French passageways as early as the 1700s, though the truth remains shades of gray, or blue. Believably cultivated by Carthusian monks, the Chartreux may have first cast copper eyes upon Paris when it emerged from a monastery outside the city. Intaking the metropolis with intrigue, the Chartreux took to the streets until it was first exhibited in 1883, across the English Channel, in a land which has yet to recognize it as a breed. This British hesitation to recognize the Chartreux is not necessarily due to questioning the breed's authenticity but more related to the great skill with which the British cultivated the blue color type and the creation of British blues. Blues have also strolled the Russian lands for centuries, in the form of a Russian blue. The first Chartreux entered the U.S. in the 1970s and was bred on French lines.

Personality Soft spoken and soft pawed well describe the Chartreux breed. Though playful and self assured, these cats are not given to claw flaunting or boisterous hollering. This is a true companion who enjoys a romp in the garden.

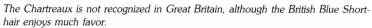

The Chartreaux is not recognized in Great Britain, although the British Blue Shorthair enjoys much favor.

Chartreaux, owned by Lenore M. Scallan.

Preferred Person   One who shall inherit the earth, a human not given to wild parties or prolonged excursions. Though not a meek breed, the Chartreux seems to fare best with the more mellow minded.

Grooming   Hardy and uncomplaining, the Chartreux typically requires little more than regular brushing and consistent attention.

Breeding   Two owner concerns are the relative uncommonness of the breed and the supreme quality demanded of show specimens (there should be no doubt of the cat's being pure and excellent).

Palatables   Meat is of the essence, balanced with other food groups; select green food purred upon. Regular meaty provisions cut to allow chewing aids in cheek development.

Proclivities & Prejudices   The breed delights in fine French art, particularly of the Impressionist period, which it finds most conducive to peaceful contemplation; though on rainy days, many a Chartreux prefers Picasso's blue period.

Colorpoint Shorthair
Siamese

Portrait

HEAD: Lengthy, with a definite taper, forming a wedge; medium in size, with good proportion to the body of great importance. Muzzle fine, also forming a wedge. Ears notably large, pointed at the tip and wide at the base, thus forming a wedge, consistent with the skull and muzzle. Eyes almond in shape, of medium size, neither protruding nor recessed; the slant of the eyes to be in harmony with the lines of the wedges formed by both the head and ears. Overall, the head is to be consistent with the requirements of the Siamese, from which the breed is derived.

BODY: Medium in size, the body is noted for its pleasing combination of the fine bone and sound (firm) muscle construction. Shoulders and hips not to disturb the sleek lines of the tubular body. Legs long and slender, with the hind legs higher than the front; both in proportion to the body. Paws oval and petite, with five toes to the fore and four to the rear. Tail long, thin, and tapering to a point.

COAT: Short, with fine texture and gloss; the coat lies close to the body.

COLOR: Body coat to be colored evenly, with delicate shading allowed but clear color preferred; contrast between body color and points of great importance to color quality. A darkening of coat is generally allowed for older cats, due to the breed's tendency to darken with age; however, contrast to remain definite between body and points. Colorpoints for the Shorthair include: red, cream, seal-lynx, chocolate-lynx, lilac-lynx, red-lynx, seal-tortie, chocolate-tortie, blue-cream, lilac-cream, seal tortie-lynx, chocolate tortie-lynx, blue-cream lynx, lilac-cream lynx, and cream lynx. Eye color is invariably a deep vivid blue.

Below: Colorpoint Shorthair, red lynx point. *Opposite:* Colorpoint Shorthair, blue-cream lynx point.

Above: Colorpoint Shorthair, red lynx point. *Opposite:* Colorpoint Shorthair, blue lynx point, owned by Alice Angermeyer.

Origin   The Colorpoint Shorthair is essentially a Siamese with points colored other than those accepted by most registries in the U.S. In the U.K. cats that would be Colorpoint Shorthairs in the U.S. are actually registered as Siamese. The dissension began when dilute mutations appeared in Siamese breeding, resulting in chocolate, blue, and lilac points. At first there was little concern, and most registries accepted these additional colors. When outcrossing to other breeds (though limited in occurrence) began and the additional color points of red, tortie, and cream occurred, many breeders curdled in defense, which in the U.S. led to a separate breed. In the U.K. these and other additional color points are recognized as Siamese.

Personality   Inquisitive and active, the Colorpoint is never at a loss to entertain itself or its owner. The breed's intelligence bares itself in every pinch. Its vocal timbre becomes well tempered through practice. Always proud, often unyielding with others of the species, Colorpoints commonly prefer not to share their immediate environment with other cats (and most dogs too).

Preferred Person   A watchful yet uncondemning human who delights in the often mischievous, seemingly ever-knowing ways of the Colorpoint.

Grooming   Caring for the coat is easy; extra attention should be given the ears, however, keeping them clean and free of detritus.

Breeding   Reaching maturity early (often at five months) and producing typically large litters (often over five kittens). Kittens are most often born whitish, with points developing later.

Palatables   The cat's svelte quality is to be maintained; therefore, both quantity and quality should be carefully measured, providing a good balance of fish, poultry, meat, vegetables, and rice.

Proclivities & Prejudices   Aloof to phosine suggestions and lurid works of Nabakov and Kafka, these cats prefer the bubble of tropical fish and flushing latrines.

Cornish Rex
Rex

Portrait
HEAD: Gently curving, the head is relatively small and narrow (length to width as one is to three), forming a medium wedge; forehead, rounded; nose break, smooth and mild. Muzzle gently tapers to a rounded backskull. Ears of large size, set high on the head; wide at their base, they taper, becoming rounded at their tip. Eyes of medium to large size, oval, with mild upward slant giving a slightly Oriental expression.

BODY: Small to medium in size, with males typically the larger of the breed. Racy in build, the torso to be long and slender, not tubular; hips well muscled, proportionately heavy in comparison to rest of body. Back to have a natural arch, with lower line of body suggesting an upward curve. Legs long, slender, typically straight. Characteristic stance is high on the leg. Paws are dainty, slightly oval in shape. Characteristically flexible, the tail is tapering, long, and slender.

COAT: Distinctive for its extremely soft and wavy quality; silklike in texture; free from *any* guard hairs. The wave of the coat has been defined as a tight and uniform marcel. The coat lies close to the body, with wave extending from the top of the head to the tail tip. Coat under the chin and on the chest and belly to be short, also with a noticeable wave.

COLOR: The Cornish Rex sports a wide range of colors, including solid even colors, chinchilla, shaded silver, smokes, numerous tabbies, tortoiseshells, calicos, creams, and bi-colors. Eye color is determined by coat color, commonly gold but green, hazel, blue, blue-green, and odd eyes (one blue and one gold of equal depth) also occur.

Below: *Cornish Rex; red mackerel tabby, owned by Nancy Mindlin.* **Opposite:** *Headstudy of Cornish Rex, van harlequin calico and white, owned by Christine W. Keightley.*

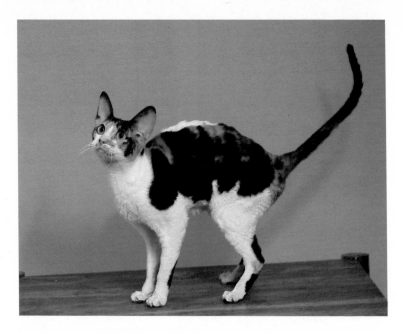

Origin   Curly-coated kittens of the Rex mutation have borne their distinctive coats in distinctive places, including Germany, Oregon, and England. Analogous to the similar mutation in the rabbit, the Rex mutation reduces guard hairs and creates a wavy coat. England is cited as the fatherland of the Cornish Rex: when a domestic specimen occurred in Cornwall, England, in 1950, it was bred back to its mother to further the mutation, thus creating a variety. Other rex mutations have occurred, producing the Devon, German, and Oregon Rexes. These varieties are considered separate, though in the U.S., the Cornish is crossed to the German, retaining the title of Cornish Rex. The Cornish Rex is the most sparsely coated of the Rex varieties.

Personality Quick in mind and body, the Cornish Rex is both the scholar and the sportsman. The breed is open-minded and responsive, delighting its owner with dexterous solutions and agile jumps.

Preferred Person The perfect gentlehuman, though allergic he may be. The refined and appreciative *sapian*, one whose mind reacts and body reflexes.

Grooming The coat has abandoned its guard hairs, and, to a large extent, the cat, its propensity to shed. Regular gentle strokes with a coat cloth (flannel or other) prove satisfactory to grooming needs.

Breeding In the U.S. the Cornish Rex has been successfully crossed to the German variety. However, the Devon and Cornish cannot be crossed without straight-haired offspring resulting.

Palatables Mutton and lamb, politely declining the mint, the Cornish Rex regards meat as "lovely." Diet should maintain, not bulge the breed's boundary in to a sunsetless domain.

Proclivities & Prejudices Small-game hunting and soft-handed forest rangers; brief but concise lectures in Western history; re-runs of the evening news.

*Opposite top: Cornish Rex, calico, owned by Irene B. Brounstein. **Opposite bottom:** Cornish Rex, van harlequin calico and white, owned by Christine W. Keightley. **Below:** Cornish Rex, brown mackerel tabby and white, owned by Catherine A. Lachenmayer.*

Cymric

Portrait

HEAD: Round; length slightly exceeding the width. Cheeks prominent; facial construction to be jowly, especially in mature males. Forehead moderately round. Muzzle well developed, less wide than long, overall giving a rounded appearance. Ears wide based, with gradual taper and rounded tips. Eyes to be large, round and full, with outer corner set slightly higher than inner.

BODY: Round and tailless, the Cymric is solidly constructed, dense, and balanced, with well-developed musculation. Chest is broad, with well-sprung ribs; back is short and forms a smooth, continuous arch. Appearing deep, the torso carries considerable flanks. Legs of heavy bone, with forelegs short and set well apart, accentuating the broadness of the chest, and hind legs much longer. Paws to be neat and round. Ideally the Cymric has a hollow at the end of its backbone in place of the set-on of a tail.

COAT: Double; medium in length, with gradual increase in length from shoulders to rump. Breeches, abdomen, and neck ruff to be longer than rest of body coat, though coat is generally long all over; lower leg and head coat to be shorter. Tufts to the toes and ears are preferred.

COLOR: Typically all colors and combinations of colors are accepted, but evidence of hybridization, in coat color or other features, is strictly forbidden. Eye color determined by that of the coat, with brilliant copper common and green, blue-green, hazel, and odd eyes (one blue and one copper) also occurring.

*Below: Cymric, red classic tabby and white, owned by Vickie L. Hansen. **Opposite:** Headstudy of Hansen's Cymric.*

Cymric, owned by Vickie L. Hansen.

Origin A true Manx, though a longhaired version of it, the Cymric occurred as a non-introduced variety in Manx litters sometime around the 1960s. The first reported specimens appeared in Canada, where continued selective breeding produced a breed true in type. Shunned by Manx breeders, Cymric fanciers established a separate breed, choosing the name Cymric to keep touch with the Celtic history of the Manx father breed. (The Manx believably began on the Isle of Man between Ireland and Wales, and *cymric* is the Celtic word for the Welsh language and culture.) Though queries about purity have been cast by Persian (Longhair) fanciers, the Cymric defends its true Manx ancestry (though the Manx itself is an obligate heterozygote) with well-documented breeding evidence.

Personality Generally active, affectionate, and likeable, the Cymric, like the Manx, tends to vary more in character than other breeds. This is reportedly due to the outcrossing necessary to these tailless breeds.

Preferred Person Flower children not turned yuppy, or at least who still pride in letting their hair grow long. Keeping with the tone of the decade of its inception, the Cymric is peaceful and all-loving.

Grooming The medium length hair keeps easily with moderate grooming, though more time is required than for a short-haired cat.

Breeding Breeding the Cymric demands good knowledge of heredity and genetics; outcrossing to Manx occurs; problems inherent in breeding with a dominant (and lethal) tailless gene present.

Palatables Keeping sweets and other shape-fudging foods to a minimum, the Cymric's diet is undemanding—typical feline meals, watching the weight.

Proclivities & Prejudices Scarves, extended polo matches, Druid folk lore and late Yeats, the strumming of the lyre, hunting lures, waiting for "Godot."

Cymric, white kitten, owned by Hansen.

Devon Rex

Portrait

HEAD: Medium length, triangular, forming a medium wedge; length to width as one is to three. Three noticeably convex curves narrow to delineate the formation of the wedge. Overall of similar shape to the Cornish Rex but with fuller cheeks, shorter nose accompanied by more noticeable stop, and larger and more widely set ears. In size the eyes are large; in shape they are oval, sloping towards the ears' outer edges.

BODY: Lean, long (rather Oriental) and muscular. Chest is broad. Legs, sturdy, carrying the body high; hind legs somewhat longer than forelegs. Paws small and oval. Tail very long and tapering, covered with fine short fur.

COAT: Of great importance. The quality of the Devon Rex's coat can be evaluated based on four criteria: density, texture, length, and waviness. The coat is densest on the back, sides, legs, tail, face, and ears; overall the cat is well covered with fur. The forehead (or temples) may be only sparsely covered. Texture of the coat is full bodied, soft and fine. Although guard hairs are present (unlike the Cornish variety) the coat is "Rexed," that is appearing to be without guard hairs. In length the coat is short, becoming shorter on the upper anatomy and chest. Waviness is most apparent on the body and tail, with a rippling effect.

COLOR: Color combinations are elaborately varied. Solids in white, black, blue, red, cream, chocolate, cinnamon, lavender, and fawn; in most solids the eyes are gold. Although not unanimously admired, bi-color, tabbies, and mottled colorations occur. The Si-Rex is a Rex showing white Siamese coloration.

Below: Devon Rex, white, owned by Bernard H. Hayduk. **Opposite:** Headstudy of Devon Rex, black, owned by Mary Theresa and Joel Singer.

Origin In the 1960s, English feline admirers worked to establish a new Rex variety. Rex fanciers were impressed to note that the Rex gene of the Devon was different from that of the Cornish, and when the two were crossed straight-coated cats were the product. While the Cornish's coat lacks guard hairs, the Devon's coat contains all three hair types, namely guard, awn, and down, but the guard hairs are typically fragile, and whiskers are often missing. The Devon's breed base has been small, which necessitates outcrossing. It was determined by breed controllers that outcrossing would cease in 1993.

Personality Fleet of foot and lively, the Devon makes an excellent pet for the owner seeking the bouncy feline. The breed is sharp of mind and sweet of nature, making it a fine companion.

Preferred Person The human who reads the book before its backcover, but never toothpaste instructions; the human not given to prejudice or assumption; the well-rounded (not to say dumpy, though sometimes balding).

Grooming Delicate stroking with a soft coat cloth, considering the delicate guard hairs, essentially fulfills the grooming requirement. The Devon Rex, lively when being groomed, may demand all the owner's patience.

Breeding Litter size ranges from three to six, with kittens quickly becoming alert and agile. Outcrossing to British and American Shorthairs, Burmese, Bombay, Siamese and Sphynx allowed before 1993. Should never be crossed to the Cornish.

Palatables Plucked goose, pheasant, and other poultry, as well as wellscaled fish and slender beefy morsels comprise the preferred menu. Meat is the vital component, keeping an eye on excessive weight gain.

Proclivities & Prejudices Trampolines and James Bond movies. Only the quickest mouse escapes (and only does so once); setting traps and feeding on pigeons in autumn.

Opposite top: Headstudy of Devon Rex, brown mackerel torbie, owned by Bernard H. Hayduk.
Opposite bottom: Devon Rex owned by Bernard H. Hayduk.

Egyptian Mau

Portrait

HEAD: Without flat planes, the head is a modified wedge, slightly rounded. A graceful contour, beginning at the bridge of the nose, is evident in profile. Muzzle is not pointed or short. The Mau's moderately pointed ears are rather large and alert, with a sheer pink tint to the inner ear. Eyes are almond shaped, big, and slant slightly towards the ears; neither circular nor Oriental.

BODY: Moderately long, with definite musculation—always in amenable balance. Legs are proportionate to the body; the hind longer than the fore. Feet are small, nearly round. Thick at the base, the tail is medium length, slightly tapering.

COAT: In texture fine and silky; a lustrous sheen is characteristic of the breed. Coat is dense and resilient, formed of medium-length hairs.

COLOR: Silver, bronze, smoke, and pewter comprise the Mau's color variations. While not commonly seen, cinnamon, blue, and lilac are presently being promoted. Silver is described as having charcoal-colored markings against a pale silver ground. Bronze is actually a chocolate tabby with brown spots over a honey-yellow ground. A white ground patterned with dark gray to black spots produces smoke. Fawn-brown with gray or brown markings warms pewter. The Mau pattern, common to all colors, insists on marked contrast between the ground and markings. Foreheads are emblazoned by clearly perceptible "M" and frown marks; a dorsal stripe, heavily banded tail, mascara-marked cheeks, and an underbelly "vest button" are characteristically celebrated.

*Below: Egyptian Mau, silver. **Opposite:** Egyptian Mau, silver, owned by Holiday Cattery.*

Origin *Mau:* Egyptian; cat. Which name could better suggest direct ties to Egypt and the ancient? In truth, the breed traces to America and the 1950s, when specimens were exported from Cairo, reaching the U.S., with passage through Italy in the royal baskets of exiled Princess Troubetskoy. Through careful selection for type and spotted coloration, fanciers achieved American acceptance for the breed starting in 1968. Today the Mau finds welcome recognition in North America and Europe, with the ever-present exception of Great Britain. Claims to the breed's direct descent from ancient Egyptian cats have been questioned, with counter claims mapping it to a wild African cat.

Personality Active and intelligent, the breed appreciates attention and is unyielding in devotion to family immediates. An agile hunter with a bird-like voice, the breed is of a truly feline nature.

Egyptian Mau, silver, owned by Holiday Cattery.

Egyptian Mau exhibiting the heavily banded tail and the characteristic "M" on the forehead.

Preferred Person   The human who rises at dawn, witnessing the glory of the sun and never questioning the power of goddess Bastet nor the cat's promise that light will erase darkness.

Grooming   Though the coat requires little more than standard shorthair grooming, the Mau remains temperamental to sudden temperature differences.

Breeding   Presents little difficulty in reproduction, but sire and dam require careful selection. Kits mature rather slowly.

Palatables   With a historical distaste for preserved foods, recalling its embalmed ancestors, Maus enjoy the home-cooked meal, American style, and sometimes pickles.

Proclivities & Prejudices   Inclined to recline in soft grass, making bird sounds, and dewinging the easily fooled species.

European Shorthair

Portrait

HEAD: Round and massive, the head is marked by well-developed cheeks. The nose is short, straight and medium in size. The chin is firm and strong. Equally developed is the muzzle. A recognizable stop beyond the whisker pads. Medium-size ears are rounded at the tips and broad at the base, always set far apart, yet completely harmonious to the roundness of the skull. The eyes are expressive and large, decidedly round.

BODY: Medium to large, the body is well put together and sturdy; the back is level; the chest broad and deep. The legs are powerful and medium-short in length. Paws round and firm. The tail, in sync with body balance, is medium in length, thicker at base and tapering.

COAT: Short, resistant and resilient—well-bodied single coat, never woolly.

COLOR: The breed displays coats of red, white, blue, black, cream, chinchillas, smokes, tabbies, patches, and bi-colors. The European Shorthair occurs in every possible color: lilac, chocolate, red, blue classic tabby, chocolate tortoiseshell, lilac tortie, blue tortie and white, and colorpoint. Tabby patterns are divided into three patterns. The classic tabby pattern is marked by broad, clearly defined dense markings. Legs are barred evenly with bracelets which stack high to meet the body. Tail is evenly ringed. The letter "M" is formed on the forehead by frown marks. The shoulder markings unfurl a unique butterfly pattern. In the mackerel tabby pattern, contrasting light and dark bands comprise the ground color. Dark necklaces; narrow leg bracelets; an unbroken dark band down the back; the tail is well ringed. The patched tabby is an established brown, silver or blue tabby with patches of red and/or cream. According to coat color, eyes can be brilliant gold, copper, green or blue-green, and hazel. Whites can occur in blue eyed, orange eyed, or odd-eyed cats; odd eyes are sapphire blue and orange, copper or golden. A blue-eyed solid white cat known as the European Albino cannot be shown in the ring, although it may be registered; the color of this albino is due to a recessive blue-eye-color gene rather than a dominant white.

Origin The definition of the European Shorthair, as a breed, is problematic in the cat fancy. Some consider the European Shorthair to be any domestic shorthair that is kept as a household pet in Europe; others consider the breed to be a British Shorthair living outside England (i.e., in Europe). The history of the European Shorthair is not unlike the history of the British cat—these vermin controllers have been associated with the Roman empire, whose soldiers promoted them around Europe to control rodent infestation. The European Shorthairs are essentially those cats that were not brought into England where later a breed standard was adopted and a new name assigned. Today many European Shorthairs trace back to the British Shorthairs since those lines were standardized first.

European Shorthair, red mackerel tabby, owned by M. Casimir, photographed in Paris, France, by Ms. Isabelle Francais in 1990.

Personality   Rugged and hardy, the European Shorthairs are untemperamental felines with great self-control. They possess quiet voices.

Preferred Person   A human with a deplorable, destroyable mouse population and a distaste for Bulldogs and certain terriers.

Grooming   A cinch. The European has strong grooming instincts and takes good care of its coat. Owners should brush these cats weekly to keep the coat shiny and clean.

Breeding   Complications are uncommon. Small litters often occur and kittens mature quickly. Crosses to British Shorthairs may be permitted.

Palatables   Meat and fish—no frills. A veritable varied palate has been nurtured by each Continental country.

Proclivities & Prejudices   Although reportedly less inclined to curtain climbing, a true European Shorthair cannot resist mounting a historical monument or ruin (especially in Greece or Rome!). Not inclined to cat shows.

Exotic Shorthair

Portrait

HEAD: Round, with good mass and very broad skull; the face too is round and is accentuated in its roundness by the nose, short and broad, and eyes, round, large, and full, set far apart, shining in brilliance. Ears rounded at the tip, not inordinately open at their base, set far apart and low on the head; they too contribute to the overall round appearance of the head.

BODY: Cobby in type, the Exotic Shorthair is low on the legs, which are both well developed and strong. Chest deep; shoulders and rump substantial. In general, size is medium to large, with quality taking precedence over size. Paws are considerably large, round and firm. Tail is typically short but must be in good proportion to the length of body; the tail is carried low to the back, on a plane, not in a curl.

COAT: Longer than the typical shorthair, the coat grows dense and plush, with a soft, believably silky texture. Coat should never be flat or lie close to the body, nor should it achieve a length at which it appears to be flowing.

COLOR: The Exotic Shorthair can be seen in almost every coat color known to cats; it can be shown in a variety of colors nearly equaling that range. Colors which are accepted in most show rings include all Persian as well as all American Shorthair colors, with the following common exceptions: golden, the Persian van bi-color, and peke-face red.

*Below: Exotic Shorthair, red classic tabby. **Opposite:** Exotic Shorthair, cream tabby.*

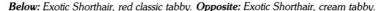

Origin   The Exotic Shorthair is a hybrid, unintentionally created through Persian-American Shorthair crosses. Throughout the middle of the twentieth century, the Persian enjoyed uncontested popularity in America. Essentially to give the American Shorthair a more "Persian" appearance, some breeders crossed the breeds. At first, these new hybrids were considered Shorthairs, but as type strayed further from the "true" American cat and, especially when the silver coat appeared, breeders realized divorce was inevitable. Under the guidance of far-seeing fanciers, the Exotic Shorthair achieved separate breed status in the latter 1960s.

Personality   Ranging from staunch independence to dependent docility, the breed is still in a state of slight flux, though forever intelligent and persevering. Prospective purchasers have little to lose: whether their kitten tends to the Persian or bends to the American, truly their Exotic will make a supreme feline companion.

Preferred Person   The reserved yet adventurous human who enjoys the pleasures of silk in the safety of the home and the challenge of staking his claim in a vast land, unknown.

Grooming   Regularly brushing the coat keeps it healthy and soft.

Breeding   Outcrossing to Persians and American Shorthairs occurs. Litter size is usually four, kittens born with darker coats which mature slowly.

Palatables   Typically unselective, the breed reportedly enjoys an occasional quick meal of the take-out kind.

Proclivities & Prejudices   Sleeping peacefully or contemplating the undulating patterns of hand-spun yarns woven to intricacy.

Exotic Shorthairs, blue smoke adult and seal point kitten, owned by Elaine Bartosavage.

Above: Exotic Shorthair, tortoiseshell kitten, owned by Benjamin Thomas. *Below:* Exotic Shorthair, blue, owned by Elaine Bartosavage.

Havana Brown
Havana

Portrait

HEAD: Longer than wide, the head forms essentially a wedge, which is more apparent in cats of the U.K. than those of the U.S. In the U.S., the face is slightly more rounded but still suggests a touch of the Orient. Of utmost importance are the narrow muzzle (appearing almost square) and distinctive whisker break; the nose tip and chin appear   nearly perpendicular. Ears are large, round at the tips, and cupped at the base; set wide but not to extreme. Eyes medium in size, oval in shape (more almondlike in the U.K.), and set wide apart.

BODY: Medium in length, taut and solid in build; neither thick nor thin, with males typically larger than females. Proportion takes precedence over size. The breed stands high on the legs, which are dainty in the female while powerful in the male. Paws oval and compact. Tail proportionate and tapering, thin but never whiplike.

COAT: Length to be short texture smooth, and appearance lustrous.

COLOR: In the U.K., all shades of chestnut brown are accepted, provided the color is without shadings; even the nose and whiskers are to be of the same uniform coloration. The paw pads, however, are pink. In the U.S., the same basic coloration is accepted, with the syntax, however, being that color tends towards a red-brown or mahogany rather than a black-brown. Eyes are green in color.

Below: Havana Brown owned by Holiday Cattery. Opposite: Headstudy of Holiday's Havana.

Origin   A self-colored chocolate shorthair, the first Havanas were registered in England in 1954. Although self-brown felines were nothing new in England, the crossing of a black Shorthair to a seal-point Siamese (which carried a chocolate gene) in the early 1950s commenced the creation of this new breed. Offspring of this litter were crossed back to chocolate-carrying Siamese, and believably a dash of Russian Blue was added to sweeten breeding practices. Members of the breed soon reached the U.S., where breeding practices differed slightly. Thus the British Havana of today appears more Siamese in type than the Havana Brown of the U.S., though they are essentially the same breed.

Havana Brown youngster.

Trio of Havana Brown kittens. Coloration darkens with age, although all Havana kittens are born completely brown.

Personality Unto itself, the character of the Havana is as distinctive as the breed's coloration. Noble yet playful, reserved but affectionate, the Havana intrigues all with its ever-inquiring mind.

Preferred Person The aristocrat given to fancy excursions, gothic tales, and inexplicably to Turkish tobacco.

Grooming Neglecting this most appealing coat is perfectly unpardonable: brushes and fine cloths shall be stroked gently, in line with the fur.

Breeding With the dam's inherent excellence in the field of motherly care, few problems to be expected. Kits are born of a lighter color shade, though still entirely brown.

Palatables Objective in its view of what enters the buccal cavity, the Havana, a hearty cat, fares well of most meals.

Proclivities & Prejudices While never fearing confrontation with the most quagmirish porcine bay, the Brown prefers to execute more civilized challenges and muddy bouts.

Himalayan
Colourpoint Longhair, Colorpoint Persian

Portrait
HEAD: With considerable mass and great breadth of skull, the head is to be round and massive. Muzzle is broad; cheeks full; nose short, with a definite stop. Ears are small, with round tips, and set with good distance between them. Eyes are large, round, and full; set far apart and not protruding.

BODY: Stocky. A build of the cobby type carried upon short, thickly structured legs. Both the shoulders and rump have good mass across the top. Overall the cat is large to medium in size. Paws large, round, and firm. Tail short but proportionate to the length of the body; carried lower than the back, straight and not curling.

COAT: Long, flowing, and offstanding on the body, with a full neck ruff continuing as a frill between the front legs, a full brush tail, and long ear and toe tufts. Texture is fine and glossy.

COLOR: Essentially a Persian with Siamese markings, the Himalayan can be seen in various pointed colorations, including a seal (cream with deep seal brown), chocolate (shadeless ivory with milk chocolate), blue (cold, shaded bluish-white with blue), lilac (shadeless glacial white with frosty gray), flame (creamy white with orange flame), tortie (creamy white with patched seal), blue-cream (shaded bluish to creamy white with blue patched with cream); other colors include chocolate solid and lilac solid (sometimes called Kashmirs). Eyes of pointed cats almost invariably a deep, vivid blue, while those of the solid colored cats typically a brilliant copper.

Below: Himalayans, flame point and seal point, owned by Gary and Karen Haddeman. Opposite: Himalayan, chocolate point.

Origin Too delicate to have scaled those mountain peaks, the Himalayan, with its eye-catching colored points, was so named because its coloration was very similar to that of the Himalayan rabbit. It is a hybrid cross between the Persian (Longhair) and the Siamese; in Great Britain and in some American registries it is known as a Colorpoint Longhair or Persian. Even today fine Persians are crossed with Himalayans to improve quality, although the Himalayan breed has "bred true" since the early 1920s. The British perfected type and recognized the breed in 1955; in the U.S. it was recognized in 1957. British fanciers exported cats to America to help exact type in the States.

Personality Composed, with a sure sense of identity. Attaches closely to one person but acknowledges other family members variously. Usually very quiet, rarely exuberantly playful; decisive, respectful and affectionate.

Preferred Person Essentially needs one human to attend to her every whim and desire—any consistent, willing soul making the mark will suffice.

Grooming Coat is extensive and needs daily attention to keep from matting. If acclimated, bathing can be undertaken with reasonable ease.

Breeding Smaller litters. Kittens attain colorpoints at about six months. Outcrosses to Persian (Longhair) permitted in certain cases. Males sexually mature considerably later than females, at about 18 months.

Palatables Balanced diet preferred; will partake of people food if so allowed, vegetables, pasta, cereal, etc., in small portions.

Proclivities & Prejudices Partial to company, whom it befriends temporarily. Disinclined towards other felines, canines generally revolting. Enjoys occasional fresh air and a chance to let down its fur in the grass.

Opposite: *Himalayan, chocolate point, owned by M. Renzacci.* ***Above:*** *Himalayan, seal point, owned by Carolyn Schwartz. In Great Britain, as well as certain American registries, the Himalayan is recognized as the Colorpoint Persian or Longhair.*

Japanese Bobtail

Portrait

HEAD: Though some variance exists, the head forms a distinct triangle, nearly equilateral in proportion, with gently curving lines. Though obviously Oriental, it is not to resemble the Siamese. Neither sharp nor blunt, the muzzle is considerably broad and rounds to the whisker break. Ears are large and broad, set wide apart at right angles to the head; they are rounded at their tips and carried upright, expressively. Eyes are large, rather oval than round, with slight slant; always bright, their color is to be in harmony with the color of the coat.

BODY: Medium, with males larger than females. Torso well muscled without being cobby, carried upon long, moderately thick-boned legs; hind legs considerably longer than forelegs, but angulated to the extent that when the cat stands relaxed its topline appears level. Paws oval. Tail characteristically short, with variance noted; reportedly can attain five inches (12.5 cm), but is often restricted to less than that length in show circles. Tail is distinctive to the breed and to each member of the breed; therefore, many tail types occur and no one should be considered most desirable.

COAT: Length medium. In texture soft and silky. Little undercoat. Shedding minimal.

COLOR: Preferred colors are black, white, and red, either as solid, bi, or tri, provided the colors are sharp and the majority of the coat is white; tortoiseshell (black, red, and cream) is also quite common. Siamese and Abyssinian colors are strictly forbidden.

*Below: Japanese Bobtail, black and white bicolor. **Opposite:** Profile headstudy of Japanese Bobtail, red, black and white tricolor, owned by Marilyn R. Knopp.*

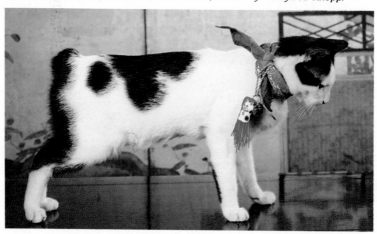

Above: *Japanese Bobtail, tortoiseshell, owned by Janet Bassetti.* **Below:** *Japanese Bobtail, tricolor, owned by Janet Bassetti.* **Opposite:** *Japanese Bobtail exhibiting the classic and often preferred tricolor pattern, known in Japan as Mi-Ke. Owner, Janet Bassetti.*

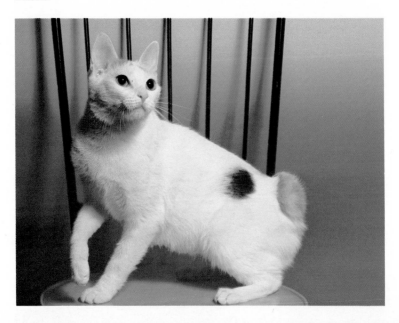

Origin Japanese imports to the United States in 1908 of bobtailed cats are the first known breed members in the Western world. It is known or thought, however, that bobtailed cats have occurred throughout the Far East for centuries. Unlike the British Manx, the Japanese Bobtail is not believed to be a mutant, with no genetic abnormality producing the bobtail. Though not very populous in the U.S. and not known in England, the breed has been recognized since 1971 in America. Servicemen brought the breed home to the States from Japan, where these cats were perceived as talismans or good luck charms, especially the tricolors known as Mi-Ke.

Personality Highly explorative and inquisitive, likes people, quite smart, generally extroverted with a defined need to be noticed and respected. Not merely an ornament around the home, this cat is a warrior on mice.

Preferred Person A candid and attention-giving human with a susceptibility to a little daily dissonance and fun.

Grooming Cat's general tidiness can be supplemented by a light brushing.

Breeding Bobtail to Bobtail matings will produce 100% bobtailed kittens; Bobtail to tailed cat will produce 100% tailed progeny.

Palatables Predisposed to seafood of all kinds; shellfish occasionally, shelled of course.

Proclivities & Prejudices The hum of a fish tank, the swish of the wind. Is not amused nor bemused by catnip. Splashes of bright colors about the house. The evening news.

Javanese

Portrait

HEAD: In type essentially similar to the Siamese. Head long, of medium size, in good proportion to the body, forming a tapering wedge. Skull flat. Muzzle fine, also wedge in shape. The overall wedge begins at the nose and, with no break at the whiskers, continues to the backskull, with allowance made for the jowls of the male. Ears very large; wide at their base and pointed at their tips. Eyes, of a definite almond shape; neither protruding nor recessed, they slant towards the nose harmoniously with the line of the wedge and ears. Of course, eyes which cross are not appreciated.

BODY: Long and svelte, dainty and of medium size. As in the Siamese, it is the appealing combination of fine bone and firm muscle that makes the winning cat. Legs are long and slender, with the hind higher than the front. Paws refined, small and oval. Tail long, thin and tapering to a point.

COAT: Essentially similar to the Balinese, except in color, the coat of the Javanese is long, with a fine, silky texture and no downy undercoat. The hair on the tail spreads to form a plume.

COLOR: All colors which are permitted for the Colorpoint Shorthair are also acceptable in the Javanese; these colors include: red, cream, seal-lynx, chocolate-lynx, lilac-lynx, red-lynx, seal-tortie, chocolate-tortie, blue-cream, lilac-cream, seal tortie-lynx, chocolate tortie-lynx, blue-cream lynx, lilac-cream lynx, and cream lynx.

Below: *Javanese, seal lynx point, owned by Andrea Fera.* **Opposite:** *Headstudy of Fera's Javanese.*

Above: *Javanese, chocolate lynx point, owned by Gail Fine.* ***Opposite:*** *Javanese, red-lynx point.*

Origin The creation of the Javanese is but a spin-off of the four-color, dancerlike Balinese. The Javanese differs from the Balinese only in color range. Beyond the Balinese's four accepted colors, the Javanese comes in sixteen colors of its own. Thus the breed offers the color range of the Colorpoint Shorthair in a longhaired variety. While the Balinese was first promoted as a breed in the mid-1940s in the U.S., the expansion into the Javanese didn't occur till much later, and was accepted by the Cat Fanciers' Association in 1987.

Personality The Javanese is an easygoing, expressive feline that naturally takes control of its master's heart and home. These are truly good cats with a positive outlook on daily life; mutual affection and appreciation are a reliable rule of paw!

Preferred Person Any cat-loving human that enjoys being spoiled by the attention of his feline housemate.

Grooming A cinch! Unlike other longhaired breeds, the Javanese requires very little dematting. A flat bristle rubber brush and a fine-tooth comb will more than sufficiently maintain the coat. Baths not necessary.

Breeding Sexual maturity is gained quite early; litter size is between three and four kittens. Allowable outcrosses were Balinese, Colorpoint Shorthair or Siamese; such outcrosses deemed no longer necessary by mid-1990.

Palatables Regular diet acceptable. Not finicky nor fussy.

Proclivities & Prejudices Moving mop heads, felt slippers; company not fawned over.

Kashmir

Portrait

HEAD: Very Persian in type, the Kashmir possesses a broad, round head; bone structure and face are perfectly round. The nose, with notable break, is short and snub. The eyes are large, round and prominent. The ears, tilting forward with rounded tips, are small and not particularly open at the base. The roundness of the head is not interrupted by the low set of the ears.

BODY: Low set and massive, described accurately as cobby—never coarse. In bone and substance, the body is markedly endowed. Muscles are well toned without suggestion of oversize. The forelegs are straight. All four are short and thick. The back is level. Paws are round, firm, of substantial size, with close-carried toes. The tail is not long, but in proportion to overall length of the trunk.

COAT: Long, vital and thick, off standing and flowing. The undercoat is notably woolly and dense. The entire body, including the shoulders, is covered by long fur, forming an immense ruff around the neck and filling out the chest and forelegs. Full brush and extensive tufts on ears and toes.

COLOR: While the Persian is seen in a kaleidoscope of colors and colorpoints, the Kashmir in color is essentially a self-colored Himalayan or solid-colored colorpointed Longhair. It is mostly seen in chocolate or lilac. The chocolate is a soft brown, a solid milk chocolate, without shading; the lilac a rich, warm lavender with a pinkish tone.

Origin A taxonomist's daydream and a superfluous breed division, the Kashmir, admittedly beautiful and striking, is but a solid-colored Himalayan or Persian. Registries that profess the Himalayan to be colorpointed as a rule do not acknowledge these longhaired cats as Himalayans. Registries that include the Himalayan as a colorpointed variety of the Persian or Longhair naturally would clump this "Persian" along with the others.

Personality Self-confident and self-colored, the Kashmir cashes in on the characteristics of the Persian. These are calm and sweet cats, with positive self-images and conceptions of who they are, even if their registries can't decide.

Preferred Person A soft-handed human who is organized and tidy, and necessarily not allergic to feline fur.

Grooming Daily intensive brushings are required to keep the Kashmir's long coat in optimum shape and avoid the cat's swallowing of fur balls, etc. Bathing can be undertaken periodically.

Breeding Newborns are fragile at birth and in need of close supervision for the first few months. Mothers often need dietary supplements to replenish their energies.

Palatables Not solely a meat diet—small portions of rice and vegetables will keep your Kashmir fit. Crunchy treats will be purred upon.

Proclivities & Prejudices Balconies with good views; linoleum and leather; solid colors; can scarcely tolerate uncouths.

The Kashmir is defined as a solid-colored Himalayan. Although most other registries consider these cats simply as Persians, the Canadian Cat Association recognizes them as Kashmirs.

Korat

Portrait

HEAD: With strong cheek development and notable broadness between and across the eyes, the head is described as being in the shape of a heart. The ridges of the eyebrows generate the upper curves of the heart, while the gently curving sides of the face complete the heart shape. Muzzle tapering; neither pointed nor squared. Stop slight. Ears rounded at their tips, flaring at their base; in general size, large. Eyes large, round, and prominent, but suggesting a slightly Oriental touch when partially or fully closed.

BODY: Neither stocky nor thin, with good muscle development, best labeled semi-cobby; medium in size. Legs of medium length, with hind legs slightly longer, in good proportion to the body. Paws oval. Tail of medium length and strong root, tapering; rounded at the tip.

COAT: Short, without undercoat, lying close to the body. In texture and appearance it is glossy, silky, soft, and fine; the coat tends to break at the spine when the cat is in motion.

COLOR: A complete silver blue, tipped with silver, without shading or tabby markings. Extensive tipping is highly desirable: the more silver tipping the better. Silver hue is accentuated where the coat is short. Silver tipping which is limited to few body parts is greatly undesirable. Nose and lips colored dark blue or lavender. Eye color preferred is luminous green but a cast of amber to the eyes is acceptable.

Origin The silver-blue, tailed talisman of Thailand, the Korat is believed to be an ancient, much celebrated Eastern cat named for the area of Thailand (then Siam) known as Cao Nguyen Khorat. For centuries the breed has been depicted in Thai poetry and paintings. Today in the Bangkok National Museum, Somdej Phra Buddhacharn Buddhasarmahathera's scroll work on *The Cat-Book of Poems*, as commissioned by King Rama V, can be admired in the Minor Arts Room, through glass, of course. It was Rama who named this handsome smooth-coated cat. In Thailand today, however, the breed is referred to as Si-Sawat (*see-sah-waht*). Believed to have been in the States since the early 1900s, the Korat wasn't accepted until the mid 1960s. In England, the breed was accepted in 1975.

Personality Highly perceptive and intelligent; gingerly approaches unknowns. With other felines, they are usually accepting but prefer the upper paw. Expressive in physical demonstration and vocalization, these are warm, mild companions.

Preferred Person Humans prone to cuddling and cooing, who enjoy quiet evenings home.

Grooming Flannel glove once-over to keep the coat resilient and clean.

Breeding Parent cats are very contemporary and share the chore of rearing the young. Slowly maturing, kittens reach adulthood by two years.

Palatables Favors poultry and other meats; less inclined to the scaled or shelled delicacies.

Proclivities & Prejudices Rock and roll is particularly loathed since the Korat finds loud noise offensive. Hates drafts, drains and drunkards.

The Korat is distinguished by its silver-blue coloration with silver-colored tips.

Longhair Scottish Fold

Portrait

HEAD: Round and broad, with chin and jaw firm. Cheeks prominent, with jowls well developed in males. The distinguishing characteristic of the muzzle is its well-rounded whisker pads. Ears are most unique, with folding, smallness and tight fold preferred; the ears are to fold forward and downward, in caplike fashion, exposing the rounded skull. The eyes are large, wide, round, and sweet in expression.

BODY: Medium in size, well rounded, padded, and even from shoulders to hips; females often slightly smaller in size. Legs, often appearing short, must have no suggestion of coarseness or restricted mobility. Toes well rounded. Tail ranges from medium to long, tapering and flexible, rarely reaching full size; tails which tend to the long and more tapering preferred; must be in good proportion to the body. Short tails with rounded tips are considered serious faults.

COAT: Semi-long and flowing, soft to the touch, persisting with much of the resilience of its shorter coated brother, the Scottish Fold. Ruff and britches are pluses.

COLOR: Blue, red, white, black, cream, chinchillas, smokes, tabbies, patches, and bi-colors. Except chocolate and lilac, the Longhair Scottish Fold wears the same coat colors as the Persian (Longhair). Tabby colors can be divided into three patterns. The classic tabby pattern is marked by broad, clearly defined dense markings. In the mackerel tabby pattern, contrasting light and dark bands comprise the ground color. The patched tabby is an established brown, silver or blue tabby with patches of red and/or cream. According to coat color, eyes can be brilliant gold, copper, green or blue-green, and hazel.

Opposite: *Longhair Scottish Fold, red chinchilla tabby and white, owned by Amy and Jean Jones.* **Above:** *Headstudy of Longhair Scottish Fold, brown mackerel tabby, owned by JoAnn Hinkle.*

Origin Despite suggestions that the Longhair variety of the Scottish Fold is not pure, no Persian or other non-kilt-wearing varmint was used in the production of the Longhair Scottish Fold. It is purported in much breed literature that longhaired kittens have long occurred in Scottish Fold litters. These cats were never standardized, possibly because the ears were nearly indiscernible. These mutations occurred in farm cats in the native land; the variant is believed to have been established through crosses between British Shorthairs and other domestics from England and Scotland. "Susie," who bended the ears of owners William and Mary Ross, is believed to be the bona fide ancestor of all Scottish Folds, no matter what the coat length. **Personality** Nosy and rugged, the Longhair Scottish Fold is solid charmer and solid survivor. These are perceptive, somewhat persistent cats with the natural ability to convince the unwilling.

Below: *Longhair Scottish Fold, brown mackerel tabby, owned by JoAnn Hinkle.* **Opposite:** *Headstudy of Amy and Jean Jones's Longhair Scottish Fold, red chinchilla tabby and white.*

Preferred Person Politically minded human who likes a challenge; should be a good talker, since Folds like to listen to chatter.

Grooming Regular brushing is essential to keep the coat clean and mat-free. The pelage isn't as long as other longhaired breeds and requires considerably less attention.

Breeding The folded ear is a simple dominant genetic mutation, thus requiring only one parent. Only 50 percent of folded ear to straight ear breedings acquire folded ears. Abnormalities can result from breeding to homozygous carrier for the folded ear. Only experienced breeders should proceed.

Palatables Haggis, hamburger, and hamhocks; puddings and heavy cream; fried mouse.

Proclivities & Prejudices Parrots (caged, of course); stamp collections; good-natured terriers; blue rooms.

Maine Coon

Portrait

HEAD: In shape, rather long with a definite squareness to the muzzle; medium in width. A firm chin and high-set cheekbones. The ears are sizable with good feathering, tapering to appear somewhat pointed, wide at the base. The eyes are set wide apart and are large; a slight slant toward the outer base of the ear.

BODY: A broad chest and a muscular conformation. In size Maine Coons are medium to large. The overall body appearance is rectangular, the body appearing long and in proportion to each anatomical component. Described as substantial, the legs are of moderate length; the paws, well tufted, are large and circular. The tail tapers and is lengthy, wide at base.

COAT: The silky-textured coat of the Maine Coon is long and flowing, giving the breed a distinctively graceful appearance. Although the coat is thick and shaggy, it rests quite naturally and smoothly on the body. Generous ruff adorning the chest is desirable; the tail is also full and feathered.

COLOR: The breed's twenty-odd coat colors can be categorized into five classes: solids, tabbies, tabby with whites, partis, and smokes. White, black, blue, red and cream comprise the solid class. Tabby patterns include classic, mackerel, and patched. Tortoiseshell and calico are but two of the possible partis. The smoke (or other) class consists of chinchilla, shaded silver as well as black, blue, cameo, and tortie smoke, among *others*.

Below: Maine Coons, kittens and adult, owned by Karen A. Jacobus, Soho Mews Cattery. Opposite: Headstudy of Maine Coon, tabby, owned by Dean Mastrangelo.

Origin This Yankee breed of feline has netted more legends to explain its origin than any other American pussy. Though unlikely, these tall tales have a unique place in American culture: the inter-species, inter-forest mating of a house cat and a raccoon; a housecat-bobcat tryst; Maine cracker barrel Captain Samuel Clough's appeasement of a French monarch's need for cuddly, furry things; a Viking transplant; overly social Norwegian Skogkatts; persuasive Russian Steppe Cats; etc. The most likely, admittedly unromantic, explanation is a cross of New England domestic house cats with imported Angoras. Angoras are generally accepted as the first long-coated cats to arrive in the U.S. Shags, as they were called in colonial times, have survived Darwin's pop-quiz and are often considered America's first show cat.

Personality Hardy and rugged, yet dignified and reserved. In the home they are responsive and never destructive; out of doors they prove enduring and resourceful working cats.

Maine Coon, red and white bicolor harlequin or van, owned by Helen M. Wohlfort. Breeders, James and Virginia Molloy.

Maine Coon, white, owned by Gerri Silverstein and Kasper Bonsignore.

Preferred Person A well-rounded human who can equally appreciate soft Dixieland at home, tree-climbing and a weekend camping, and unexpected late-night excursions.

Grooming The thick, full coat of the breed needs human intervention to keep it up. Regular brushings remove dead hairs and make the coat more manageable for the cat to primp. Constant grooming is not required.

Breeding Males particularly prepotent; females often require encouragement. Kittens number two or three and do not mature fully until four years of age.

Palatables Hearty appetites for meat and fish. Fresh-caught cod and lobster are never refused.

Proclivities & Prejudices Balancing on hind legs and butting heads with a consenting human are noteworthy proclivities; loves to be outdoors, amenable to long stories on rainy nights.

Manx
Cat of the Isle of Man

Portrait

HEAD: Well-developed cheeks indeed dominate the Manx's semi-round head (the head is more long than it is broad). The cheek bone pronunciation is considerable; undoubted jowliness lobbies for a debatably round appearance. The whisker break is noted. A strong chin and prominent muzzle. The eyes are large and full. The ears appear rounded at their tips without extensive tufting.

BODY: Sturdily constructed, good bone and musculation create a compact and well-balanced feline. A broad chest and well-sprung ribs facilitate a stout physical conformation. The legs are strongly boned and italicize the deepness of the chest. Hind legs to be much longer than fores. Paws neat and round, as a cat's should be. Taillessness is essential to be a Manx: "a decided hollow at the end of the back where, in the tailed cat, a tail would begin" (CFA standard).

COAT: The thick double coat of the Manx is short and dense. The undercoat, in texture and feel, will resemble cotton. The outer coat is quite long and open, not silky, since the desired coat quality is more important than its color or pattern.

COLOR: The Manx possibilities for color are many. Since hybridization is always an important consideration, any color or pattern that would suggest a Himalayan connection is not allowed; chocolate and lavender, in some circles, would point to a hybrid and are therefore not permitted. A glimmer of the Manx rainbow: white, black, blue, red, chinchilla, blue smoke, silver patched tabby, cream tabby, calico and tortoiseshell.

Opposite: *Manx, tortoiseshell and white, bred and owned by L. Alice Hanbey.* ***Above:*** *Headstudy of Manx, brown mackerel tabby, owned by Raymond R. Freiberger.*

Origin The olympic-swimming Samson or the hasty, door-slamming Noah have often been pooled to explain the genesis of Manx. The Bible does not detail Samson's de-tailing of the sea-faring feline, who had shorter locks than the longhaired Babylonian; likewise, the Bible also doesn't account for the accidental amputation of the rat-killing Manx before the Ararat arrival. Other legends tell of Irish warriors adorning their helmets with cat tails (a la Davy Crockett?) and of Phoenicians or the Spanish Armada sailing these cats from the Orient to the Isle of Man. Nevertheless, these *stubbin* (tailless) cats have been known on the Isle for centuries.

Personality *Stubbin* though not stubborn, the Manx is a resilient and ruddy feline, with a keen ability to adjust to its environment. They are typically shy yet personable, clever though endearing. Hell-givers to mice and other small rodent types.

Preferred Person A discriminating human willing to share his home; Manx are affectionate to all members of the human family.

Grooming Coat is soft and should not be overbrushed, though regular attention is surely advised.

Breeding Reproduction is endowed with serious considerations: Manx kittens can be born with a lesser or greater degree of tail; continued breedings of tailless to tailless can lead to vertebrae malformations; crosses to Manx with embryonic tails can alleviate certain potential problems.

Palatables Red meat and cheese are favored; unapproving of fish, unless caught by itself.

Proclivities & Prejudices Unpredictable reactions to water; Celtic music; particularly disturbed by slamming doors.

Opposite: Manx, brown classic tabby. **Above:** Manx, black, owned by Marjan Swantek. **Below:** Manx, black and white bicolor, bred and owned by L. Alice Hanbey.

Nebelung

Portrait

HEAD: Wedge shaped. The skull is flat on top and long. The wide set of the eyes, which are rounded in shape, give the face a broad appearance. The nose is of moderate size. The ears are large and wide at the base, with marvelously rounded tips. They are rather translucent in appearance due to the thinness of skin and absence of noticeable feathering.

BODY: Without indication of coarseness, the body outline is graceful as is the carriage. Overall it is fine boned and long; musculature is firm and apparent. The legs are comparably fine in bone and long in length. The slightly rounded paws are small. The tail begins quite thickly at the base and tapers over its notably long length.

COAT: Medium–long on the body; the tail is adorned with hair no shorter than that on the Persian.

COLOR: While a clear, even, bright blue is of course this Russian's only color, the preferred shade varies from place to place. In the United States, the color is desired in lighter shades; in England, a medium blue is preferentially desired. A deep green eye color is characteristic of the breed, no matter what shade the coat color.

Origin A Cinderella story, the history of the Nebelung traces to an abused black female cat named Terri, who gave birth in the early 1980s to one litter of two black females and a male who appeared to carry Angora blood. One female, named Elsa, was mated to a male who looked like a Russian Blue. The litter produced six solid-colored black and blue kittens. A second mating to the same male produced an additional seven kittens. A male (Siegfried) from the first litter and a female (Brunhilde) from the second litter were acquired by Cora Cobb. Both these cats displayed medium-long hair and a plumelike tail. Through the careful matings of Siegfried and Brunhilde, Cora Cobb created the breed known today as the Nebelung. In September 1987, the breed received TICA recognition. With unwavering persistence and dedication, Ms. Cobb continues to propagate this most promising breed.

Personality Affectionate and loving, the Nebelung delights family members with its adaptability, intelligence, and overall pleasing demeanor.

Preferred Person The observant human who gives a smile, a kindly stroke, a warm word of love.

Grooming Not given to matting or shedding, the Nebelung's coat demands little time from the owner. A daily once-over adds sheen and suits the basic grooming needs.

Breeding Because it is a breed in transition, the Nebelung should be mated with caution and strict adherence to the breed standard, neutering

Nebelung, blue, owned by Cora Cobb, founder of this exciting new breed. This longhaired blue beauty is Romani Pralo of Nebelheim, bred by foundation breeder John Hruza. The sire was Nebelheim Loki of Romani ex Nebelheim Zuphie of Romani.

those cats which do not conform. Litter size varies from one to six, with three to four being most common.

Palatables   Never fussy and always accommodating, the Nebelung enjoys variety; an occasional "people treat" will not corrupt its diet.

Proclivities & Prejudices   Summers in Moscow, anything endless by Wagner, Norse folktales, Chicago cat exhibitions.

Norwegian Forest
Norsk Skaukatt

Portrait

HEAD: Round and substantially big. The eyes are oval shaped and slant toward the outer base of the ears. The forehead appears wide, as the ears are set high and well apart. The nose is of medium-long length. The chin is firm and well aligned with the nose and upper lip.

BODY: The muscular, broad-chested conformation of this Norwegian cat is quite similar to the Maine Coon Cat's. It is medium in size, males tending toward large. The legs are firmly boned; the paws large and round. The heavily coated tail is longish and more dramatically plumed than the American cat.

COAT: Thick and insulating, a double coat made to wear with little wear—a woolly undercoat, outer coat is generally long throughout, though often shorter on shoulders. Notably abundant frontal ruff.

COLOR: Tabbies, solids, bi-colors and parti-colors all occur. Essentially all colors are permitted. The thickness of coat and soundness of physical construction have always been more important than color.

Below: Norwegian Forest, blue torbie and white, owned by Joselyn Aalbu. **Opposite:** Headstudy of Norwegian Forest, brown classic tabby and white, owned by Jane Barletta.

Above: *Norwegian Forest, blue torbie and white, owned by Joselyn Aalbu.* **Opposite:** *Norwegian Forest, brown mackerel tabby, owned by Jane Barletta.*

Origin   Adding to Norse fables the attraction of feline mystique, the Norwegian Forest unquestionably antedates most modern breeds of cat. Enchanted, the breed was first recognized in 1930, as the single native cat of Scandinavia. The breed has survived the harsh wilds and icy winters of its native land for centuries. Not unlike the Maine Coon cat, the Norwegian Forest is adorned by a profuse coat, which sheds as the summer months encroach. The breed is not registered in Great Britain and finds small numbers outside its native land. Though kissed by the breed's mysterious origins, intrigued and desiring companions realize that their own land is plentifully stocked with more easily accessible cats.

Personality   Sharp in intelligence, the Norwegian Forest is ever-conscious of its environment: he is alert, suspicious, and never fearing. As a feline counterpart, the breed excels for those desiring a little more of the untampered feline spirit.

Preferred Person   The hardy, rugged human who practices the art of individualism yet, unhesitating, yields a helping hand to his tried neighbor.

Grooming   The dense coat, shedding in the warmth, surprisingly asks for little human care. Essentially self-sufficient, he grooms himself. Occasional combing services him.

Breeding   Propagating for centuries, often in the wild, where Darwinism is felt most, the breed poses little reproductive difficulty.

Palatables   The owner should provide the well-balanced feline diet and not be surprised if the Forest opts for a paw-picked critter instead.

Proclivities & Prejudices   Fireplace mantels, sudden drafts, *Tannhaüsser* on Saturday mornings, and the call of the puffin are all pleasers.

Ocicat

Portrait

HEAD: A modified wedgelike skull curves slightly from the broad muzzle to cheeks, which should not appear too full. Considerable length and squareness are appropriate to the Ocicat skull. The eyes are moderately large and set apart well; they should angle slightly upward. The ears are quite large for the size of the skull, always standing erect, cornering the top of the head. They are set at a 45-degree angle with ear tufts vertically aligning the inner sides of the ear cups.

BODY: An athletic, solid frame which is rather long-bodied, deep and full—coarseness and bulkiness are to be avoided. Slightly sprung ribs and good depth of chest; the back is somewhat higher towards the rear. The legs are medium long and substantially muscled; feet oval and compact. The tail is longish, slim and tapers towards its dark-colored tip.

COAT: Short and sleek, lying quite close to the body yet long enough to accommodate the desired agouti coloration. The fur is fine in texture; woolly coats should be put to pasture, as they are undesirable.

COLOR: Vital and most important is the distinctively spotted agouti pattern of the Ocicat. The face is colored lighter than the rest of the body; the tail tip, the darkest. Twelve colors are possible, and each should be clear and amenable. The tabby pattern is necessarily free from blotches, with scattered, defined spots throughout the body being essential to the proper pattern. Contrast is paramount as well. Six shades of silver (silver, chocolate, cinnamon, blue, lavender and fawn); tawny, a brown tabby; chocolate; cinnamon, a soft brownish; blue; lavender or lilac; and fawn comprise the twelve colors. Eye color can be any color other than blue; deep colors preferred.

*Below: Ocicat, silver, owned by Rebecca Nan. **Opposite:** Ocicat, silver.*

Above: *Headstudy of Nan's Ocicat.* **Opposite:** *Ocicat, cinnamon.*

Origin   The Ocicat is a hybrid breed which has resulted from crosses of Abyssinians, American Shorthairs, and Siamese. The Ocicat was recognized by the CFA in 1987 and is named for the South American wild cat called ocelot, whom it resembles. Presently the only outcross allowed by registries is the Abyssinian, and all outcrosses were ruled to cease on January 1, 1995. This continued Aby-only breeding has considerably added to the tendency of the foreign in the breed, possibly leading to an increasing physical resemblance to the Egyptian Mau. Ocicat fanciers have focused on the future as their breed base solidifies and their supporters mount.

Personality   Active and athletic in mind and body, the Ocicat is the true sportsman, thriving with fresh air and new challenges. The breed has been labeled an attention getter, clearly revealing   Aby ancestry. Siamese traits can be witnessed in the breed's watchful, attentive moments.

Preferred Person   The human who enjoys full-bodied taste, cold-filtered beer, and cream the way it used to be: un-ultra-pasteurized.

Grooming   Minimal care in the way of brushing and combing, with simple, regular procedures.

Breeding   To keep the spots from blotching, only the finest breeding specimens should be employed. As with any "new" hybrid, breeder caution is paramount.

Palatables   Undemanding, though steamed vegetables, with plenteous meat, served on a light bed of rice may be purrferred.

Proclivities & Prejudices   This ambassador is fond of percussion and large masks, silk fans and pillows, bad Nixon jokes, Churchill memoirs, and candlelight prayer services.

Oriental Longhair

Portrait

HEAD: A flat skull contributes to the long tapering wedge of the head; the line from the top of the head to the tip of the nose is straight and unbroken, without a lift over the eyes or indentation over the nose. The ears are very large and pointed, with lines continuing the plane of the wedge. The eyes are almond shaped and of moderate size, quite prominent but not protruding. Crossed eyes are incorrect.

BODY: Sleek, long and muscular. The abdomen is tight, hips and shoulders contribute to the sleekness of line. The legs are slim and lengthy; hind higher than fore. The tail, which is thin at its base, is also lengthy, and tapers to a defined point.

COAT: Medium length, dense and resilient. The tail is quite extensively plumed, though not to the extent of the Persian.

COLOR: This cat comes in solids, shaded colors, tortoiseshell, smoke and tabby. The shaded colors overcast blue-cream silver, cameo, chestnut-tortie, cinnamon silver, lavender-cream silver, as well as others. Smokes in blue, cameo, chestnut, ebony, fawn, lavender, cinnamon, and even parti. All tabby patterns and possibilities are viable and acceptable. Eye color is most commonly and preferredly green; white cats may have either blue or green eyes; odd-eyes never acceptable.

Below: Oriental Longhair, shaded chestnut spotted tabby, owned by Marjorie A. Bergen. Opposite: Oriental Longhair, fawn mackerel tabby, owned by Bergen.

Oriental Longhairs, shaded chestnut spotted tabby and fawn mackerel tabby, owned by Marjorie A. Bergen.

Origin　The Oriental Longhair apparently is an outgrowth of the Oriental Shorthair—quite a plush, glorious outgrowth at that. The notion of developing a longhaired variety of a popular shorthaired breed is not new to the cat fancy, and has been accomplished in many breeds. Most often a Persian cross is utilized to gain the desired coat length and type. Such longhaired versions are undeniably elegant and maintain the sleekness and delicacy of their shorthaired cousins.

Personality　Truly winning and consistent, the Longhair ranks among the most sensitive feline companions; it is sometimes considered an extremist (in personality and instincts).

Preferred Person　Any human with time to share and still wearing a mood ring.

Grooming　Never extensive, though more demanding than its Shorthaired counterpart. Daily brushings are beneficial.

Breeding　Outcrossing to the Shorthair is still permitted. Typical litter size is three or four.

Palatables　The breed's lean build makes the need for low-cal Oriental meals unnecessary. Affinity for mackerel confessed to by some breed members.

Proclivities & Prejudices   Late art deco and bad Andy Warhol sketches are favored; well-woven rugs to sleep on and a passing Shorthair to cuddle with.

Headstudy of Bergen's Oriental Longhair.

Oriental Shorthair
Foreign Shorthair

Portrait

HEAD: A flat skull contributes to the long tapering wedge of the head; the line from the top of the head to the tip of the nose is straight and unbroken, without a lift over the eyes or indentation over the nose. The ears are very large, strikingly so, and pointed, with lines continuing the plane of the wedge. The eyes are almond shaped and of moderate size, quite prominent but not protruding. Crossed eyes are incorrect.

BODY: Tubular—sleek, long and muscular. The abdomen is tight; hips and shoulders contribute to the sleekness of line. The legs are slim and lengthy, hind higher than fore. The tail, which is thin at its base, is also lengthy, and tapers to a defined point.

COAT: Close lying, short and fine textured. In appearance, the coat should be glossy.

COLOR: This cat comes in solids, shaded colors, tortoiseshell, smoke and tabby. In both the U.S. and U.K., all variants except the solids, which are perceived in Great Britain as individual breeds, are acceptable for the Oriental Shorthair. The solids, blue, chestnut, cinnamon, cream, ebony, fawn, lavender, red, and white (as well as caramel in the U.K.) are labeled foreign shorthairs. The shaded colors overcast blue-cream silver, cameo, chestnut-tortie, cinnamon silver, lavender-cream silver, as well as other pleasant-sounding, handsome hues. Smokes effervesce in blue, cameo, chestnut, ebony, fawn, lavender, cinnamon, and even parti. All tabby patterns and possibilities are viable and acceptable. Eye color is most commonly and preferrably green; white cats may have either blue or green eyes; odd eyes never acceptable.

Below: Oriental Shorthair, white, owned by Dean Mastrangelo. ***Opposite:*** *Oriental Shorthair, blue-cream silver.*

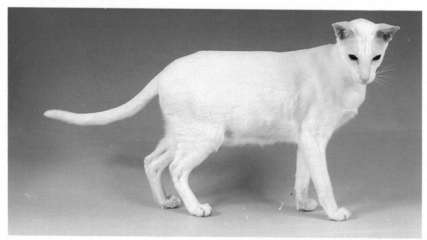

Origin In the U.S. the Oriental Shorthair breed includes all Siamese which cannot be registered as either Siamese or Colorpoint Shorthairs; thus it includes shades, smokes, tabbies, and partis. In the U.K. only tabbies, torties, and spotted tabbies are considered Orientals, for self-colored Siamese are designated as foreigns, each receiving separate status. The first Orientals appeared as Siamese color mutations in Great Britain in the 1950s, as breeders strove to produce the Havana. Importations soon reached the U.S., where additional mutations were added to the ranks of ever-growing Oriental registrations.

Personality Discriminate best describes the Oriental's character: it considers carefully the time, the place, and the person who will receive its exuberance, its arrogance, its affection, and its disdain. The total of the breed's personality far exceeds the sum of its color possibilities.

Preferred Person The human of strong character, never afraid to pose off-color.

Grooming Essentially trouble-free, though the cat's chosen person is best to execute all (weekly) grooming procedures.

Breeding Although keeping colors clear in the mind can be difficult and/or tiresome, the breed typically has few mating or birthing complications.

Palatables A connoisseur of the East: home-prepared sushi, an occasional stirfry, and crisp snowpea pods provide indelible delight.

Proclivities & Prejudices Hates doors; keen on screens and large insects; sneers at imitators, occidental deli owners, and all-things kitsch.

Opposite: Oriental Shorthair, ebony, owned by Marcella and Ronald Syminiuk. **Above:** Oriental Shorthair, red tabby, owned by the Syminiuks.

Persian
Longhair

Portrait

HEAD: Imposing, broad and round; bone structure and face is perfectly round. The nose, with notable break, is nearly peke-like, short and snub. The eyes are large, round and prominent. The ears, tilting forward with rounded tips, are small and not particularly open at the base. The roundness of the head is not interrupted by the low set of the ears.

BODY: Low set and massive, described accurately as cobby—never coarse. In bone and substance, the body is markedly endowed. Muscles are well toned without suggestion of oversize. The forelegs are straight. All four are short and thick. The back is level. Paws are round, firm, of substantial size, with close-carried toes. The tail is not long but in proportion to overall length of the trunk.

COAT: Long, vital and thick, off-standing and flowing. The undercoat is notably woolly and dense. The entire body, including the shoulders, is covered by long fur, forming an immense ruff around the neck and filling out the chest and forelegs. Full brush and extensive tufts on ears and toes.

COLOR: Among the most popular colors seen are: solids or selfs in white, black, blue, red, cream, blue-cream, and smokes; chinchilla, a white coat tipped with darker colors; smokes in black, blue, cameo, tortoiseshell, or blue-cream; tabby patterns; bicolors, a color and white; patched coat patterns; and colorpoints in chocolate, tortie, lilac-cream, flame, seal, blue, and others. Eyes can be brilliant copper, a deep vivid blue, green, blue-green, or odd.

Opposite: *Persian, blue tortie, owned by Carol and Melinda Duncan.* ***Above:*** *Persian, blue-cream, owned by Marianne Lawrence, Insta-Purr Cattery.*

Origin Persians believably descend from the long-coated Turkish cats called Angora. Both regarded simply as Eastern cats, the early Angoras and Persians shared little distinction between them, though the Persians had denser, more woolly coats. The Persians were favored by Europeans for their coats, and concentrated breeding efforts further beatified the breed and all but extinguished longhaired competition. The Turkish cats were virtually to disappear from the scene until the twentieth century. The continued growth of Persian appeal has also affected such unshakingly popular breeds as the British and American Shorthairs in their native countries: such is the allure of the Persian, a breed of renowned fancy and recognition.

Personality Though consistent in love of family and friend and unquestionable in potential as the premier house cat, the Persian is not likely the easiest of purebreds to adopt: affection is not always solicitable. Intelligent and demanding.

Preferred Person Ye who open your heart to the Longhair shall not escape unmoved: though the Persian has a preferred person, it acknowledges the attention of all its admirers—for a while.

Grooming Daily, thorough brushing is imperative: too many ingested hairs can cause intestinal upsets. Employ a natural bristle brush and gentle touch. Dry shampoos are preferred unless necessity dictates otherwise.

Breeding Kittens demand extensive maternal care for about 16 weeks. A very sound diet, with supplements recommended, is imperative for the dam through the course of her pregnancy and maternity.

Palatables Too much fat and excessive carbohydrates are to be carefully guarded against. A balanced, varied diet, with a good protein level, is best for the breed. Vitamin and mineral supplements often prove useful during the first year.

Proclivities & Prejudices Undoubtedly *the* indoor/apartment cat, the Persian's paradise includes woven wool, fragrant spices, and priceless jewels.

Opposite: Persian, smoke tortie, owned by Cindy Swartz. **Below:** *Persian, black and white bicolor.*

Ragdoll

Portrait

HEAD: Round with prominent, well-developed cheeks. The nose is straight and of medium size and length. The ears are on the small side; they are pointed and angle at 45 degrees towards the tip. The eyes are roundish and may incline slightly.

BODY: The body's tendency to go limp when handled is no indication of lack of substance or musculation. Of good length and quite solid, the Ragdoll is a big cat with an imposing presence.

COAT: Medium long to long in length, the coat is silken in texture; the neck is adorned by a heavy ruff; the ear tufts are not as impressive as the Persian's.

COLOR: Three "brands" of Ragdolls by color are available: cats with white mittens, cats without white mittens, and bi-colors. The mittened and mittenless are indeed colorpoints. In color, as opposed to pattern, colorpoints can be seal, chocolate, blue, cinnamon, fawn, and frost (lilac). Bi-colors are most often in combination with white. Eyes are blue in color.

*Below: Ragdoll, blue point mitted, owned by Georgann Chambers. **Opposite:** Headstudy of Ragdoll, frost bicolor, owned by Linda Swierczynski.*

Origin Soft thunder showers of controversy boom upon the breed, in part due to a flaccid explanation adhered to by some fanciers. That the breed traces to an auto-struck female White Persian (Longhair) may stand to inquiry, but that she passed her limpidness as acquired from shock of the accident falls short of satisfying the genetic minded. This flaccidity is bred for in laboratory mice, a quality conducive to scientists' handling of the specimens; it is admittedly a curious feature in a purebred cat. As best can be determined, the Ragdoll was developed during the 1960s in America. The exact component stock remains undocumented, which has slowed the recognition process considerably for the breed. Registration acceptance didn't begin until the mid-1980s; not all American registries recognize the breed.

Personality Selective breeding has yielded in the Ragdoll a cat of infinite docility and gentleness. Mild-mannered and affectionate, the Ragdoll was named for its proclivity to go "soft" when stroked—even by the most tactfully stimulative hand.

*Above: Ragdoll, frost bicolor, owned by Linda Swierczynski. **Opposite:** Headstudy of Ragdoll, chocolate point, owned by Swierczynski.*

Preferred Person   Well-stuffed, though not stuffy, Anns and Andys, as tranquil and tender as the cats themselves, include the Ragdolls favored humans.

Grooming   Mollification with the brush, graciousness with the hand: regular soft brushing keeps the coat healthy.

Breeding   Limp when handled and generally meek, the breed is not the most prolific of breeders, but so long as type and especially temperament are strongly considered little difficulty should be present.

Palatables   Can be picky, particularly at picnics, where picking is tantamount to good manners; truly a meat eater, though tea parties are characteristically favored.

Proclivities & Prejudices   Refuse to chase white mice; known to pounce upon unattended pies; perusal of lost and founds and personals cannot be precluded.

Russian Blue

Portrait

HEAD: Wedge shaped. The skull is flat on top and long. The wide set of the eyes, which are rounded in shape, give the face a broad appearance. The nose is of moderate size. The ears are large and wide at the base, with marvelously rounded tips. They are rather translucent in appearance due to the thinness of skin and absence of noticeable feathering.

BODY: Without indication of coarseness, the body outline is graceful as is the carriage. Overall it is fine boned and long; musculature is firm and apparent. The legs are comparably fine in bone and long in length. The slightly rounded paws are small. The tail begins quite thickly at the base and tapers over its notably long length.

COAT: Dense and silky to the touch, the coat is double and plush, though quite short. Resilient and fine, it stands up from the body.

COLOR: While a clear, even, bright blue is of course this Russian's only color, the preferred shade varies from place to place. In the United States, the color is desired in lighter shades; in England, a medium blue is preferentially desired. A deep green eye color is characteristic of the breed, no matter what shade the coat color.

Below: *Russian Blue, owned by Laura M. Moody.* **Opposite:** *Headstudy of Moody's Russian Blue.*

Above: *Russian Blue, bred by Natalie Del Vecchio and owned by Catherine Rowan.*
Opposite: *Russian Blue youngster poses with the czar.*

Origin Like most other cats that derive from days long ago and places far away, the exact origins are blurred, and the Russian Blue is no exception. It is purported that the breed was imported into the United Kingdom by Elizabeth I from the Russian port of Archangelsk; for a time, the breed was known as the Archangel cat. During the breed's early British show career, it was known as the Foreign Blue. The arrival of various blue shorthairs to the States is dated in the early 1880s; Sweden and England are cited as the exporters of American Russian Blue lines. This handsome and sweet cat has been accepted throughout much of Europe and North America.

Personality   Serene and independent, these are unintrusive but demonstrative felines. Quick witted, acrobatic and resourceful.

Preferred Person   An apartment-dwelling human who enjoys his independence as much as his cat does; a human perceptive enough not to disturb his cat at inopportune moments.

Grooming   Grooming is minimal and should not be overdone; hair should be brushed so that it stands erect.

Breeding   Pure breed lines are essential to sustain the desired consistent coloration; four kittens per litter is average.

Palatables   Amenable to most offerings, small quantities often favored; caviar is unfortunately too salty for these native Russians.

Proclivities & Prejudices   Tidy apartments, soft jazz, a place to hide; dislikes unexpected guests; fancies plants and high balconies.

Scottish Fold

Portrait

HEAD: Round and broad, with chin and jaw firm. Cheeks prominent, with jowls well developed in males. The distinguishing characteristic of the muzzle is its well-rounded whisker pads. Ears most uniquely folding, smallness and tight fold preferred; the ears are to fold forward and downward, in cap-like fashion, exposing the rounded skull. Eyes, large, wide, round, and "sweet" in expression: beckoning, trusting.

BODY: Medium in size, well rounded, padded, and even from shoulders to hips; females often slightly smaller in size. Legs, often appearing short, must have no suggestion of coarseness or restricted mobility. Toes well rounded. Tail ranges from medium to long, tapering and flexible, rarely reaching full size; tails which tend to the long and more tapering preferred; must be in good proportion to the body. Short tails with rounded tips are considered serious faults.

COAT: Short, dense, soft and resilient.

COLOR: Blue, red, white, black, cream, chinchillas, smokes, tabbys, patches, and bi-colors. The Scottish Fold wears the same coat colors as the American Shorthair. Tabby colors can be divided into three patterns. The classic tabby pattern is marked by broad, clearly defined dense markings. In the mackerel tabby pattern, contrasting light and dark bands comprise the ground color. The patched tabby is an established brown, silver or blue tabby with patches of red and/or cream. According to coat color eyes can be brilliant gold, copper, green or blue-green, hazel, or odd.

Scottish Fold, calico, bred and owned by Karen A. Votava.

Scottish Fold, black and white bicolor, owned by Linda Swierczynski.

Origin The shepherd's occupation has historically allowed for observation of glorious sights: a star in the East, a canine controlling the flock with its eyes, and a barn cat with folded ears. On a farm near Coupar Angus, in 1961, in the Tayside Region of Scotland, William Ross, a watchful shepherd, spotted a feline; her ears folded forward and downward. She carried a dominant genetic mutation, which through selective crossings to British Shorthairs created the Scottish Fold breed. Exports to Australia and the U.S. proved successful, and the breed was quick to take hold of hearts of cat fanciers around the world. The breed today enjoys international recognition and appreciation, though remaining relatively small in number.

Personality Sweet and affectionate, the Scottish Fold delights the owner with its resilient adaptability: from farmyard backyard to condo terrace, the Fold proves companionable and undemanding—and forever the mouse thwarter.

Scottish Fold, red mackerel tabby, owned by Terry Havel.

Scottish Fold, tricolor, owned by Judith A. Nelson.

Preferred Person Though unbiased and unconditionally accepting, the Fold does prefer the shepherd type—watchful and protective, one human among the animals.

Grooming In addition to normal shorthaired brushing, an eye must be focused on proper tail and foot development; inflexible tails, thick legs and feet, and splayed toes are all serious warning signs.

Breeding Erect-eared cats are essential to all breeding practices. The dominant gene for folding has been associated with dysplasia and other malignant conditions. Outcrossings to American and British Shorthairs (guarding against loss of type) are employed. Don't expect all kittens to display folded ears.

Palatables Not always partial to native dishes, the Fold cannot resist a good haggis especially prepared for it.

Proclivities & Prejudices Batting a mouse is more than a game. Good conversation, the drone of a radiator or musette, lawn sheep, wet wool, rugged landscapes.

Siamese

Portrait

HEAD: Wedge shaped, long and tapering; medium in size, in excellent proportion to the body. Beginning at the nose, the wedge, in forming a perfect triangle, continues to the ears, with no break at the whiskers; allowance is made for the more prominent jowls of the male cat. Neck elegant. Muzzle fine, long, smoothly merging into the foreskull; its shape is wedge. Ears set well apart, large, wide at their base, tapering to a pointed tip; the ears are to continue the lines of the wedge. Eyes Oriental: almond-shaped, slanting towards the nose harmoniously with the lines of the wedge and the ears; the distance between the eyes should not exceed the width of one eye.

BODY: Medium in size; svelte in build (fine in bone, firm in muscle); refined, with tapering lines. Shape is termed tubular: shoulders and hips in line with the torso. Legs slender; hind of greater length than fore. Paws refined, small and oval. Tail long and thin, tapers to a fine point.

COAT: Lying tight to the body, the coat is short, fine, and glossy.

COLOR: Pointed; in the U.S., four colors are commonly recognized; in the U.K., eight additional colors are commonly accepted. In the U.S, a Siamese of a color recognized in the U.K. but not recognized in the U.S. as Siamese is designated as being a Colorpoint Shorthair. In other words, the eight Siamese colors recognized in the U.K. which are not accepted in the U.S. are accepted in the U.S. under the Colorpoint Shorthair breed. Self-colored Siamese are recognized as Oriental Shorthairs in the U.S. and foreign shorthairs in the U.K. However, whereas all Oriental Shorthairs   are self-colored Siamese, not all foreign shorthairs are self Siamese. The four Siamese colors in the U.S. are: seal point (pale fawn to cream, shading to underparts, with deep seal brown); chocolate point (unshaded ivory, with milk chocolate); blue point (bluish white, shading to white underparts, with deep blue); lilac point (unshaded glacial white, with frosty gray of pinkish tone). Additional colors recognized in the U.K. are: tabby point, tortie-tabby point, red point, seal-tortie point, blue-tortie point, chocolate-tortie point, lilac-tortie point, and cream point. Eyes always to be a deep vivid blue.

Opposite: Siamese, blue point. The four classic
Siamese points include the seal point, chocolate
point, blue point and lilac point. The breed's eyes,
regardless of point color, are always deep vivid blue.

Left: Siamese, lilac point,
owned by Larry Levy.
Below: Siamese, chocolate
point, adult and kitten,
owned by Irene B.
Brounstein.

Origin Within them the souls of en route nobles, Siamese protected spiritual temples and homes of royalty for centuries in their native Thailand (Siam). Revered, Siamese were not permitted in the hands of commoners. The first Siamese to enter England were likely the King of Siam's gifts to Owen Gould, English Consul-General. These cats reached England in the early 1880s. Their Crystal Palace appearance generated energetic enthusiasm unceasingly. The first Siamese in America likely traveled a similar route: King of Siam's gifts to First Lady Mrs. Rutherford B. Hayes, via Consul David Stickles, in 1878. With uninhibited appeal, Siamese mastered the feline fancy. Outcrossings and selection for color mutations have created numerous other Siamese-related breeds, including the Colorpoint Shorthair, Javanese, and Ocicat, to name but a few.

Siamese, blue point. The Siamese conformation is required to be svelte and refined, with tapering lines.

Personality   Some believe that character is consistent with color, differing as colors differ: the seal point, more extroverted; the blue-point, more affectionate; while the chocolate point is more lighthearted and funloving. All Siamese are watchful and intelligent; they are what they are when they wish to be so. (As any cat will tell you.)

Preferred Person   The worldly experienced, cultured, and knowing—the human secure, undoubting, true.

Grooming   With a propensity towards profuse seasonal shedding, Siamese require daily brushing to remove dead hairs and clean and beautify the coat.

Breeding   Females mature early (often at five months), and litters are typically large. Early and over-breeding can endanger the dam. Poor health and bad physical condition are not to be tolerated in the breeding program.

Palatables   The feline preference for fish is an over-rated truism to which the breed has innocently contributed. Seafood, steamed or broiled; no affinity generally for shellfish, unless handfed. Siamese generally do enjoy fish, which food is helpful in keeping the trim figure of the cat. Fats and excess to be avoided.

Proclivities & Prejudices   The mysterious butterfly resting on the foreskull, or painting such a portrait.

Singapura

Portrait

HEAD: Round in skull and width; tapering at the the outer eye to the definite whisker break. Muzzle broad; nose blunt, with a straight line formed from it to the chin. Ears are large, wide at their base, slightly pointed at their tip; they are set at a medium distance on the skull. Eyes too are large and moderately almond in shape, showing a slight slant. Small eyes and/or ears are not tolerated.

BODY: Small to medium in size, with sound muscle and bone development; males typically weigh around six pounds (2.7 kg), while females average around four pounds (1.8 kg). Overall construction to be square: body length and shoulder height equal in distance. Legs heavily boned and strongly muscled. Feet small and oval. Tail round at its tip, slender, not too thin; in length, not to reach the shoulder when laid across the back.

COAT: Exceptionally short, slightly longer in kittens. Fine in texture, it is to lie close to the body.

COLOR: Singapore has sent no color separations for the breed to the U.S.: all Singapuras have an ivory ground color ticked with dark brown. "Unbleached muslin" is the CFA's designated color for the muzzle, chin, chest, and stomach. Nose leather pale to dark salmon. Highlights (eyeliner, nose outline, whisker apertures, between the toes) to be dark brown.

Singapura, ticked brown, owned by Juli McAllister.

Headstudy of Singapura owned by Hugh Richbourg.

Origin   First recognized in America in 1988 by TICA and CFA, the Singapura is a very old breed of Singaporan origin—Singapura being the Malaysian name for the island nation we call Singapore. Referred to as a street cat, the breed in its native land exhibits a wide spectrum of color. Speculators predict that the breed is on the move and that additional colors are soon to be recognized. Hal and Tommy Meadow stake their claims as being the first to bring the breed to the U.S., "finding" specimens in 1974 and bringing them "home" in 1975. An additional Singapura was retrieved for the Singapore SPCA in 1980, which also contributed to American breeding stock.

Personality   From the people-packed streets of Singapore, the Singapura holds no fear of man, though the breed may tend to reserve affection for those it knows well. A stranger in a strange land, the cat is inquisitive, ever investigating the sound of a microwave or the instigative roar of a vacuum cleaner.

Preferred Person   The human who is open-hearted and open to suggestion, patient and willing to share his home and its secrets (mechanical and spiritual) with even the most unapologetic of felines.

Grooming   Easycare, the breed fares well with moderate brushing and stroking.

Breeding   Adaptive and hearty, the Singapura poses little breeding difficulty, though a limited breed base poses its ever-probable problems—over breeding, high prices, etc.

Palatables   The breed has so long subsisted on whatever was available that its tastes are open to most foods. Some cats have oddly acquired the taste for zucchini ice cream.

Proclivities & Prejudices   The breed has a great liking for color, and is believed to be able to separate one from another. No dislikes reported; strong favoritism for Miniature Poodles.

Opposite: Singapura, owned by Tord and Suzanne Svenson. Though the major registries do not accept colors other than flecked brown, other colors do occur in Singapore and will undoubtedly begin to appear in the Western world.

Snowshoe

Portrait

HEAD: Broad, round and strong. Cheeks are full; muzzle rounded. Chin is strong and well developed. Rounded at the tip, the ears are medium in length; they are broad based and set well apart. Eyes are roundish is shape, with the outer corner tipping *ever* so slightly upward.

BODY: Long and well developed; the legs are thick set and medium in length; the paws are large, round, and firm. Tail is medium in length and proportioned well to the body.

COAT: Despite its arctic-seeming name, the Snowshoe's fur is short, not substantial enough to rough the ice and snow. It is silky in texture.

COLOR: The Snowshoe gracefully has stepped into the Himalayan coat coloration with either blue or seal points. The white markings on the feet travel as high as the ankle on the forefeet and the hock on the hind. The muzzle, also white, ideally is marked by an inverted "V"—a blaze or a white chin is also acceptable. The eyes are from a rich teal to turquoise.

Origin Considered an "experimental" breed or a breed in progress, the Snowshoe is a hybrid, created through the crossing of a Siamese and a bi-colored American Shorthair. The first generation of this cross will not exhibit the desired colorpoints and therefore must be crossed back to another hybrid of similar genotype or the Siamese to produce correctly colored progeny. At one time, the appearance of the Snowshoe could be said to vary from anywhere between the very foreign (Siamese) and the very domestic (American Shorthair). Hard work and regimented breeding efforts have done much to refine type and promote the breed.

Personality In general, the Snowshoe is docile and affectionate, with the inclination towards extroversion and inquisitiveness inherited from its Siamese relations. Easygoing and adaptable, they make fine companions.

Preferred Person Though the name and mittens may indicate otherwise, the warm human who enjoys cocooning makes the ideal counterpart.

Grooming The short coat asks for little time, thus leaving plenty for affection and play.

Breeding Requires a knowledge of genetics and an eye that discerns. Stock must be chosen carefully with regard for genes both carried and displayed.

Palatables Hot toddies, snowcones, and other usual dietary supplements.

Proclivities & Prejudices The Oriental/American: small cars, quality cameras, and micro-electronic gadgetry raise ears of interest.

Opposite: Snowshoe, owned by Doris-Chinn Reese.

Somali

Portrait

HEAD: Modified wedge, slightly rounded, tapering to the muzzle. Muzzle is gently contoured, congruent with the shape of the skull, never sharply pointed or snipy. Ears large, broad at their base and moderately pointed at their tips; set back on the skull and held alertly. Eyes large, almond in shape, bright and expressive; importantly, the dark lidskin, which is surrounded by a lighter colored area, is to accentuate the eyes. Above each eye is to be a short dark vertical pencil stroke, with a dark pencil line continuing from the upper lid towards the ear.

BODY: Refined yet strong, medium long, with a moderately rounded back. Ribs well rounded. Legs slender yet sturdy and of good substance; proportionate to the body in length. Feet oval and compact. In general, the Somali should appear light of foot, quick and agile. Tail thick at base, tapering slightly, fur-covered to form a full brush.

COAT: Medium length (only moderately longer than the Abyssinian), double, soft and very fine. Dense coats are preferred, as are ruffs and breeches. Ear tufts possible.

COLOR: Often compared to the Abyssinian, the Somali comes in blue (soft blue-gray, ticked with slate blue; ivory undercoat; tail tipped slate blue; underbody and forelegs cream to beige); ruddy (orange-brown ticked with black; underbody and inner legs even ruddy); and red (red ticked with brown; deeper shades preferred). Invariably, eye color is gold or green, with richness and depth appreciated.

Below: Somali, ruddy, owned by Margary S. Hoff. **Opposite:** Headstudy of Somali, ruddy, owned by Abby C.A. Carbine.

Above: Headstudy of Somali kitten, owned by Carolyn S. Goldberg. **Opposite:** Somali, owned by Abby C.A. Carbine. Breeders are presently experiencing much success with new colors in the Somali breed. However, blue, ruddy, and red are the only accepted colors in most registries.

Origin The 1960s saw the creation of a longhaired variety of the Abyssinian. As did the Balinese (longhaired Siamese), the Somali brought immediate inquiry and dissension to the father-breed's fancy. It is argued by some but denied by many that Persian/Longhair blood was infused to create the Somali. Regardless of the politics, however, the Somali has attained unquestionable recognition since its creation. Somalis are so popular as pets and as show cats that potential owners face waiting lists to acquire their chosen breed of cat.

Personality The Somali is said to share all the desirable characteristics of the Aby but reassembled in the beauty of a long coat. Adaptable and accepting, Somalis are often the cat of choice for owners with other cats or pets.

Preferred Person The devout human, one not given to stray or straggle, resistant to hagglers.

Grooming The longhaired, double-coated cat requires consistent grooming to keep it soft and tangle free.

Breeding The longhaired gene is autosomal recessive. When crossed to the Abyssinian, all offspring will be shorthaired but carry the longhair gene.

Palatables Not given to cake, the Somali cries: let me eat meat.

Proclivities & Prejudices Never given to flaunting its fine fur, the Somali feels particular distaste for cold and prefers the cozy warmth of its master's corduroy.

Sphynx

Portrait

HEAD: Rather small relative to body size, not too triangular. The ears are, however, quite triangular, with a suggestion of roundness at the tips. Noticeable curvature towards the muzzle; cheeks flat. The eyes are oval and incline outwards. The chin is small and strong.

BODY: Conformation is lightly muscled; body is slender overall, but appears more so as a result of the absence of coat. The legs are of medium length; the tail is long without tapering notably.

COAT: Coatlessness, essentially, is singular to this breed of cat. Actually, very short hair on the face, ears, paws, testicles, backbone and tail gives the cat a suede-like feel. Some Sphynx are born coated yet still carry the hairlessness gene. Additionally, the breed is whiskerless, in most cases. Facial hair on some specimens may be longer than in others; these cats may have some semblance of whiskers as well. Fur on the tails in some cats is even noticeable at first glance.

COLOR: Despite this essential lack of coat, the Sphynx can be any color, solids, tabbies, and others, since pigment still remains in the animal's cells. Eyes can be golden, green, or hazel.

Below: Sphynxes, black and white bicolor and red and white, owned by Sandra Adler. Opposite: Headstudy of Sphynx kitten owned by Lisa Bressler.

Origin   Hairless mutations have intrigued the animal world for generations—the African Sand Dog, the Chinese Crested Dog, and in 1966 the Sphynx breed of cat. In Canada, in an otherwise normal litter of otherwise typical domestic cats, a hairless kit appeared. The mutation sparked fascination, and breeders promoted the breed to the extent that it received Canadian recognition, which in the end proved short lived. Sphynx are not all born completely hairless; many kits are covered with short hair that sheds with age. Warm controversy continues to bundle and befuddle the breed, and this is not likely to subside in the near future.

Personality   Like pre-apple Adam and Eve, playful and unashamed, unaware of its nakedness, the Sphynx maintains the pure feline character which has endeared the race to multitudes from time incalculable. Unabashed, the Sphynx looks onward to a time when man resides unbiasedly.

Sphynx, owned by Lisa Bressler.

Sphynx, red and white, owned by Sandra Adler. The Sphynx appears in any coat color, including solids. tabbies, and torties.

Preferred Person   Candid and loving, the Sphynx never sinks to apology: its human of preference is he who looks for no explanation when indeed there is no need for one.

Grooming   Though brush-free the breed makes demand in the form of special skin care. To guard against the elements, lotion should be applied. In addition, mouse nips and rat scratches are to be avoided at all cost.

Breeding   Because the gene for hairlessness is recessive, it can be carried for generations by coated individuals, only to evidence itself at the most untimely breeding. Responsibility must be employed.

Palatables   No artificial flavors or colors for this true-to-the-skin feline; only fresh meats served regularly appease the appetite.

Proclivities & Prejudices   Exclusive beaches, sweaters for Christmas, Bermuda exhibitions and exhibitionists, and Bearded Collies.

Tonkinese

Portrait

HEAD: With more length than width, the skull forms a modified wedge. A break at the nose is noticeable. The cheekbones not prominent; profile clean with marked contours. Muzzle is blunt, with a slight whisker break. Moderate sized ears, with oval tips, are broad at their base. Eyes are oval, slightly rounded at the bottom, creating an essentially open appearance; they are wide set.

BODY: A beautifully proportioned Tonkinese refrains from the svelte, elongated Siamese body type, while resisting the cobby influence of the Burmese. This perfect feline medium is balanced and muscular without coarseness. The legs are fairly slim; hind longer than fore. Paws are less round than oval. Tail tapers and is proportionate to the medium-length body.

COAT: Lustrous to the eye and silky to the touch, the coat is close-lying and medium short in length.

COLOR: The breed is richly wardrobed in five shades of mink: natural mink, medium brown with lighter hues, with darker points; champagne mink, a

*Opposite: Tonkinese, owned by Jean Bernstein of Shotoku Tonkinese, the originator of the Tonk breed. **Above:** Headstudy of Tonkinese owned by Sheila L. and Martha S. Reams.*

buff cream with medium brown points; blue mink, a bluish-gray with slate blue points; honey mink, described as a golden cream with an apricot cast, with ruddy brownish points; and platinum pink, a light silver-gray, with pewter gray points. Harmonizing gracefully with the ground color, dense points are required on the mask, ears, feet and tail. Deep, clear and brilliant, the eyes are aqua in color, without exception.

Origin An American creation of the 1960s, the Tonkinese represents a Siamese-Burmese cross that strives to balance perfectly the "better" points of each breed. Physically situated in the middle, more cobby than the Siamese and more lithe than the Burmese, the breed captivates (and accumulates) fanciers throughout North America—the breed enjoys recognition in both the U.S. and Canada. This is a hybrid which has fast gained the respect of purebred cat fanciers. In Great Britain, however, the breed has not gained recognition, largely because the Siamese and Burmese are not as different as they are in America.

Personality Well-adjusted to their just deserts, Tonks are outgoing and confident. Communication with their humans is second nature. Never enraptured by their own rapturous appearance, these cats are alluring and often provoke applause. Their antics, curiosities, and good nature make them exceptional pets, rarely in need of guidance or reprimand.

Preferred Person A flexible, level-headed human, not given to daily routines or normalcy; fairness punctuated by lapses of fun preferred.

Grooming Regular or irregular brushings. Should a Tonk entangle itself in taffy or torte, don't hesitate to bathe it well (with or without its approval).

Breeding As a hybrid breed, Tonks produce litters with "variants," that is, pointed kittens with white or off-white coats, or even solid-colored coats. These non-mink-colored variants are perfectly normal otherwise, but are exempt from show ring participation.

Palatables A balanced feline diet supplemented by self-acquired sherbets and tropical compotes.

Proclivities & Prejudices Acrobatic contortions are the norm; certain breed propaganda purports that Tonks behave like eagles—the authors have fallen upon unfortunate firsthand experience indicating that Tonks *cannot* fly.

The Tonkinese exhibits five shades of mink, each of which is pointed and attractive.

Tonkinese, owned by Larry Rhinard.

Turkish Angora
Angora

Portrait

HEAD: Wedge shaped, tapering towards the chin in a straight line, with jowl allowance in the male. Nose straight, forming an unbroken line with the foreskull. Ears of good length, wide base, and pointed tips; the ears are set highly and held alertly. Eyes large, almond in shape, slanting slightly towards the nose.

BODY: Medium and of fine bone, with males slightly larger. Torso long and balanced, with rump riding slightly higher than the shoulders. Legs long, with hind legs longer than fore. Paws are small and round. Tail long and tapering, carried lower than the body but not to drag; carried over the body when in motion, nearly touching the skull. Tail forever fully coated.

COAT: Medium long on the body; long at the ruff. Neck, belly and tail (full brush) are thickly coated. Tufts to the ears. Texture fine and silky. Unlike the Persian, undercoat non-existent.

COLOR: Traditionally pure white, the Angora is accepted in a variety of colors. In the U.K., all colors recognized for foreign shorthairs are also acceptable for the Angora. Common Angora colors include: black, blue, chocolate, lilac, red, tortie and calico, cream, blue tortie, chocolate tortie, lilac tortie, tabby (all colors), smokes and bi-colors. Eye colors depend upon coat color and include amber, blue, green, hazel, and odd-eyed (one blue and one amber); amber is the most common eye color.

Below: Turkish Angora, white, celebrating its well-woven ancestry. Opposite: Head-study of Turkish Angora, tabby, owned by Maria Carpolongo.

Turkish Angora, white.

Turkish Angora, owned by Maria Carpolongo.

Origin The ancient Angora breed derives from the Pallas cat which was domesticated by the Tartars and Chinese, and later perfected in Ankara, Turkey, hence the name Angora. These fine longhaired cats are the progenitors of the ever-popular Persian (Longhair) breed. It is believed that indiscriminate crossings between the Angora and the Persian led to a lack of purity in the former breed. Fortunately, the Ankara Zoo in Turkey thankfully has been propagating a line of the breed, keeping it pure. The cats were imported and promoted in the United Kingdom during the 1950s and sparked attention in the United States about a decade later.

Personality These gentle and kind cats enjoy time spent with their owner. While some breed members tend toward shy or aloof, others are notably outgoing and gregarious.

Preferred Person A well-balanced human who has room in his life (and home) for an affectionate feline.

Grooming Daily grooming sessions, somewhat extensive, are obligatory to keep this bountiful coat soft and silky.

Breeding Kittens do not develop full bloom of coat until about two years. Some propensity for deafness in blue-eyed white cats, as in the Persian breed, also applies here.

Palatables Commercially prepared cat food is most fit for this well-adjusted modern feline. Some prefer the milk of the mohair goat.

Proclivities & Prejudices Snubs small-talkers and artificial friends—this genuine feline is not tolerant of lesser characters; fancies Mozart comic operas, gymnasts, and the hum of the dishwasher.

Turkish Van

Portrait

HEAD: Wedge shaped, tapering towards the chin in a straight line. Ears of good length, wide at their base, and pointed at their tips; the ears are well covered with hair and show a typically pinkish tone. Eyes large and essentially almond in shape.

BODY: Fine in bone and medium in size, with males slightly larger. Torso long and balanced, with rump slightly higher than the shoulders. Legs long, with hind legs longer than fore. Paws are small and round. Tail long and tapering, carried lower than the body but not dragging; carried over the body when in motion, nearly touching the skull. Tail profusely coated.

COAT: Medium long on the body; long at the ruff. Neck, belly and tail (full brush) are thickly coated. Tufts to the ears. Texture fine and silky. Unlike the Persian, undercoat non-existent.

COLOR: A chalk white marks the ground color of the Van. Auburn markings over the eyes (on the forehead) interrupt an otherwise solidly colored white body; the tail is also auburn, with lighter and darker rings adorning it. Eyes are typically amber, but blues also occur. A cream or off-white ground is reportedly in the works, although acceptance has not yet been attained.

*Below: Turkish Van, owned by Frank Szablowski. **Opposite:** Turkish Van, owned by Barbara and Jack Reark, Matabiru Turkish Vans.*

Headstudy of Turkish Van owned by Frank Szablowski.

Origin While not promoted specifically in the Lake Van district of Turkey, the first two specimens of the Van breed were located in that area. Two tourists, Laura Lushington and Sonia Halliday, took the two foundation cats home to Britain in 1955. These two white cats with piebald markings were derived from Turkish Angoras and were bred to establish their coat pattern in a breed of cat. Today there is some dissension as to what constitutes the perfect Van pattern; most concur that less than 25% pied is desirable. Cat breeding in Turkey was never as color-specific as American and British fanciers have always made it out to be.

Personality Highly independent and yet still affectionate to all human charges. This is a smart but not a show-offish cat that enjoys play without losing control.

Preferred Person A reserved human, content to be blessed by the companionship of a fine animal; demonstrative persons often favored.

Grooming Daily brushings are necessary to keep the coat in optimum shape.

Breeding Though not prolific breeders, no complications readily surface, excepting the preservation of the desired coloration.

Palatables Naturally inclined to fish but will accept quality meat products with a little encouraging.

Proclivities & Prejudices These ex-lake-dwellers, sometimes called "swimming cats," are enamored by water, yet not all are swimmers, willingly; dripping sinks and tubs are particular favorites.

The "swimming cat" has received its name for crystal clear reasons. This is Matabiru Lady Mac Beth at four months wading among the lily pads in the Reark's garden pond.

Appendix I:
The Longhairs

Breed Name	Origin	Registries
American Curl (longhair)	United States	C.C.A., T.I.C.A.
Balinese	United States	C.C.A., T.I.C.A., C.F.A.
Birman	Far East	C.C.A., T.I.C.A., C.F.A., G.C.C.F.
Colourpoint Longhair	Great Britain	G.C.C.F.
Cymric	North America	C.C.A., T.I.C.A., C.F.A.
Exotic Longhair	Canada	C.C.A.
Himalayan	Great Britain	C.C.A., T.I.C.A., (G.C.C.F.)
Javanese	United States	C.F.A.
Kashmir	Canada	C.C.A.
Longhair	Middle East	G.C.C.F.
Longhair Scottish Fold	United States	T.I.C.A.
Maine Coon	United States	C.C.A., T.I.C.A., C.F.A.
Nebelung	United States	–
Norwegian Forest	Norway	T.I.C.A.
Oriental Longhair	United States	T.I.C.A.
Persian	Middle East	C.C.A., T.I.C.A., C.F.A., (G.C.C.F.)
Ragdoll	United States	C.C.A., T.I.C.A.
Somali	United States	C.C.A., T.I.C.A., C.F.A.
Turkish Angora	Turkey	C.C.A., T.I.C.A., C.F.A., G.C.C.F.
Turkish Van	Turkey	T.I.C.A.

C.C.A. Canadian Cat Association (Canada)

C.F.A. Cat Fanciers' Association (United States)

T.I.C.A. The International Cat Association (United States)

G.C.C.F. Governing Council of the Cat Fancy (Great Britain)

Parenthesis around a cat associations initials indicates that the breed is recognized in that registry by a different name.

Balinese on the line with C.F.A.

Cymric.

Himalayan.

Maine Coon.

Persian.

Persian.

Norwegian Forest.

Somali.

Appendix II:
The Shorthairs

Breed Name	Origin	Registries
Abyssinian	Egypt/Ethiopia	C.C.A., T.I.C.A., C.F.A., G.C.C.F.
American Curl (shorthair)	United States	T.I.C.A.
American Shorthair	United States	C.C.A., T.I.C.A., C.F.A.
American Wirehair	United States	C.C.A., T.I.C.A., C.F.A.
Bengal	United States	–
Bombay	United States	C.C.A., T.I.C.A., C.F.A.
British Shorthair	Great Britain	C.C.A., T.I.C.A., C.F.A., G.C.C.F.
Burmese	Far East	C.C.A., T.I.C.A., C.F.A., G.C.C.F.
California Spangled	United States	–
Chartreux	France	C.C.A., T.I.C.A., C.F.A.
Colorpoint Shorthair	United States	C.C.A., C.F.A.
Cornish Rex	Great Britain	C.C.A., T.I.C.A., C.F.A., G.C.C.F.
Devon Rex	Great Britain	C.C.A., T.I.C.A., C.F.A., G.C.C.F.
Egyptian Mau	United States	C.C.A., T.I.C.A., C.F.A.
European Shorthair	Continental Europe	–
Exotic Shorthair	United States	C.C.A., T.I.C.A., C.F.A.
Foreign Shorthair	Great Britain	G.C.C.F.
Havana Brown	Great Britain	C.C.A., T.I.C.A., C.F.A., G.C.C.F.
Japanese Bobtail	Japan	C.C.A., T.I.C.A., C.F.A.

Korat	Thailand	C.C.A., T.I.C.A., C.F.A., G.C.C.F.
Malayan	Far East	–
Manx	Isle of Man	C.C.A., T.I.C.A., C.F.A., G.C.C.F.
Ocicat	United States	C.C.A., T.I.C.A., C.F.A.
Oriental Shorthair	Great Britain	C.C.A., T.I.C.A., C.F.A., (G.C.C.F.)
Russian Blue	Soviet Union	C.C.A., T.I.C.A., C.F.A., G.C.C.F.
Scottish Fold	Great Britain	C.C.A., T.I.C.A., C.F.A.
Siamese	Thailand	C.C.A., T.I.C.A., C.F.A., G.C.C.F.
Singapura	Singapore	C.C.A., T.I.C.A., C.F.A.
Snowshoe	United States	–
Sphynx	Canada	T.I.C.A.
Tonkinese	United States	C.C.A., T.I.C.A., C.F.A.

C.C.A. Canadian Cat Association (Canada)

C.F.A. Cat Fanciers' Association (United States)

T.I.C.A. The International Cat Association (United States)

G.C.C.F. Governing Council of the Cat Fancy (Great Britain)

Parenthesis around a cat associations initials indicates that the breed is recognized in that registry by a different name.

Abyssinian.

American Shorthair.

Bombay.

Chartreux.

Manx.

Scottish Fold.

Singapura.

Index